Face to Face

Face to Face
*Interviews with Leo Rangell,
Arnold Richards, and Estela Welldon*
Volume I

Moisés Lemlij

International Psychoanalytic Books (IPBooks)
New York • http://www.IPBooks.net

Published by IPBooks, Queens, NY
Online at: www.IPBooks.net

Copyright © 2020 Moisés Lemlij

All rights reserved. No part of this book may be used or reproduced in any manner whatsoever including Internet usage, without written permission of the author.

ISBN: 978-1-949093-58-2

For Mimi, Maia, Alec, Micaela, and Camila

Contents

Foreword to the American Issue by Moisés Lemlij ix

Leo Rangell 1

Arnold Richards 69

Arnold Richards's Afterword 146

Estela Welldon 148

Estela Welldon's Afterword 209

Foreword to the American Issue by Moisés Lemlij

I owe the idea of publishing this book to my wife, Mimi. After reading Philip Roth's interviews with several writer friends in *Shop Talk*, she suggested that I conduct similar interviews with psychoanalysts from different countries and schools of thought, in which they could talk about their lives, their professional careers and their ways of understanding psychoanalysis. The more I mentally reviewed the number of interesting friends and colleagues I could interview, the more enthusiastic I was about the idea. In that first moment, it seemed a relatively simple adventure. Gradually however, complications began to appear: from whom to interview, to what order and how to coordinate the itinerary of my trips for professional or personal issues with the agendas of my interviewees, to how to coordinate the process of recording, transcription and editing of the interviews, many of which would have to be translated before being published. Nonetheless, I fully immersed myself in this project which has spanned several years and during which time I have been able to count on the constant encouragement of Mimi and the support of my collaborators Dana Cáceres and Pedro Cavassa.

During the first two years I spent time conducting interviews with colleagues from different continents as I met them on my trips. It became clear that the interviews would require three or four long sessions and considering distance and language, the most practical plan of action was to complete a first volume of interviews with Latin American psychoanalysts. In the next couple of years that followed, I planned some trips with the exclusive purpose of meeting with essential personalities and I devoted my efforts to finishing the transcription and editing of their interviews. This allowed me to complete and publish the first two volumes of *Face to Face* in Spanish in 2011 and 2017, respectively.

As the reader will appreciate, I did not have a list of structured questions going into the interviews, I allowed the 'yarn' of the conversation to unravel naturally. It is also evident that the tone, rhythm and content of our conversations bear traces of the history and characteristics my relationship with the interviewees; which I would like to now briefly summarise.

I had already heard of **Leo Rangell** and read some of his work when I met him for the first time in Lima in the late 1970s. I lived in London then and while on vacation in my hometown I took the opportunity to attend a few seminars offered by Leo. At the time, he was a member of the committee appointed by the International Psychoanalytic Association (IPA) to sponsor the psychoanalytic study group that gave rise to the Peruvian Psychoanalytic Society. We had a great connection and we continued to keep in touch. After a while we started seeing each other regularly over several years, at the meetings of the Executive Council of the IPA. He attended first as Honorary Vice-President and then as Honorary President, and I was there initially as Latin American Secretary, then as Vice President and finally in the role of Treasurer. On such occasions we were always able to get away for a while to catch up and talk about different topics, particularly about psychoanalytic theory and institutional politics, coinciding on many thoughts. I also had the privilege of him accepting my invitation to give the opening speech of the International Conference 'At the Threshold of the Millennium' sponsored by the IPA and UNESCO that I organized in Lima in 1998.

Needless to say, Leo was one of the first people that came to mind when I thought about who I should interview. I took advantage of the opportunity to stay a few more days in Los Angeles to interview him when I was invited to participate in a congress of the Peruvian American Medical Society, an organization that brings together 1,500 colleagues. Leo recommended that I stay at a hotel near his home, and he would arrive to collect me driving his car even though he was 97 years old by then. That first day he took me out to eat and followed our meal with a guided tour of the homes of his notable neighbors -including the late Marylin Monroe- before we went to his house. We spent four unforgettable days talking together. A few months later, I was very saddened by the news that he had died. His death also meant that he was unable to review the transcription of our conversations, and/or complete some of the passages or correct some of the names mentioned, which made the task of editing difficult and lengthy.

One of the Latin American psychoanalytic personalities that I could not overlook interviewing and that I have also included in this first volume in English, because most of her career has been carried out in England, is **Estela Welldon**, my professor, colleague and dear friend who Mimi and I consider part of our family. I met her in London in the mid-1970s, when we were both at the Portman Clinic, a center of excellence for the psychoanalytic treatment of sexual disorders and antisocial behavior. I was still at the training level and had to report on my work to Estela, with whom I learned so much discussing cases. It was then that the very close professional and friendly relationship that has lasted until today began. She has come to Peru many times, where she has a large number of followers who are interested in developing her ideas on female sexuality and perversions. In addition, I have been invited by her to more than one congress of the International Association of Forensic Psychotherapy, an organization she founded and of which she is the Honorary Life President. We meet in London a few of times a year now as Mimi and I travel regularly to visit our daughter and our granddaughters, giving us the opportunity to also enjoy Estela's warm hospitality.

I met **Arnold Richards** and his wife Arlene when they came to Lima in 1994 to participate in the Latin American Congress of Psychoanalysis chaired by Saúl Peña, then president of the Latin American Psychoanalytic Federation (FEPAL). A Clinical Meeting in Cusco followed, which gave us the opportunity to get to know each other better and build on our friendship. Later, I saw them more than once in Washington D.C., where we also met with Louis and Nancy Goodman, very good mutual friends, as well as in various congresses of the IPA or the American Psychoanalytic Association

(APsaA). Arnie and Arlene also accepted my invitation to come to Lima to participate in the International Conference 'At the Threshold of the Millennium' in 1998.

In addition to the admiration I have for his superb and innovative tenure as editor of the Journal of the American Psychoanalytic Association, I am connected to Arnie by Yiddish -our mother tongue that has allowed us to go to see a Yiddish play together in New York- and by our common leftist Jewish roots. In fact, he provided me with very valuable information about the American branch of my family, especially Clara Lemlich, the famous union and feminist leader. Due to his remarkable career as an editor, his contributions to theory and his institutional work, I had no doubt that I should interview Arnie. He accepted immediately when I proposed it to him, and he invited Mimi and I to his beautiful house in Upstate New York where we spent delightful days and had long conversations while we walked through the woods. Arnie not only agreed to be one of my interviewees, he was also very interested in my editorial project. So much so that the fact that this corrected and augmented American edition of *Face to Face* will see the light is due largely in part to his enthusiastic initiative and active collaboration, for which I am most grateful.

The experience of conducting these interviews has been enormously rewarding and enriching. Beyond the different professional and life experiences of each one of my colleagues, past their different ways of conceiving psychoanalysis and their particular interests, there is something which I find difficult to define that we all have in common; it is no accident that they are also my friends. It has been deeply moving to discover, or rediscover, different facets of myself through them. I trust that readers will enjoy these interviews as much as I did.

Leo Rangell

You have received a lot of people here. How come Wilfred Bion was a year in Los Angeles and didn't come to see you?

You didn't know that? He would even be surprised to hear this, if he were alive. He never came to see me because, I guess, I was reputed to be someone who doesn't fall for something that's not common sense. You know, wispy thinking, treating metaphors as though they are realistic. There was one occasion during that year, when he was introduced with great fanfare by a person who was to me questionable in the first place. He was the one who brought Hanna Segal, Herbert Rosenfeld, and Donald Meltzer, the whole Kleinian movement in London to Los Angeles, during a time of great upheaval in this city. Privately, and he had a great rivalry with me, a guy named Bernard Brandschaft.

That was in the sixties?

It was the late fifties and the early sixties. I was president of the American [Psychoanalytic Association] in the early sixties and in the middle sixties and aroused great malignant envy. Not benign envy, which is normal and helpful, but to the point of very great hostility and acting out and divisiveness and polarization of the membership. This was known as the place between Ralph Greenson and Leo Rangell.

When you read his textbook there's nothing wrong. It's good, it's a model textbook almost. It's what people should do. The quarrel between me and Greenson was never between me and his textbook, it was between me and what he did. Like for example the famous one.

Marilyn Monroe.

Who died right down the street here, one block down [from] here.

So, you had very famous neighbors…

Greenson was a black eye to psychoanalysis all the way through. He had her in his house, talk about transference. Transference was supposed to be some attempt to be neutral and objective but here such attempts were given up because the rationalization was that she was a borderline or psychotic so therefore he was following the technique of a guy named Milton Wexler.

I am writing all about that now in another connection. I am explaining the whole history of psychoanalysis in LA [Los Angeles] and how it affected psychoanalysis throughout this country and therefore throughout the world. This used to be the area of so-called 'ego psychology'. Americans liked to call it psychoanalysis or ego psychology. I always point out that it's a complete misnomer and another one of these short-hand, misconceptions that leads people in the wrong direction. American psychoanalysis was never ego psychology. It was always id, ego, super ego, internal world, external world, psychoanalysis, psychosynthesis. And it's labelled, [in] shorthand, 'ego-psychology'.

Why?

Because it followed id psychology. Following World War II, we all came back from the army exultant, triumphant. We had introduced psychodynamics into psychiatry, and the psychodynamics was a treatment. My theoretical ideal was Otto Fenichel, that's the textbook to me. It was not Greenson but Fenichel. Greenson was Fenichel's patient. Fenichel was here in LA [Los Angeles]. I met him, the whole thing is an amazing history, it could be a Broadway play because Freud sent Fenichel to LA. He also sent Ernst Simmel to LA.

I first heard of Fenichel's text when I was a resident in psychiatry in New York City and this text was coming out chapter by chapter in the Psychoanalytic Quarterly. And I was a resident, not in psychoanalysis but in psychiatry, and I began to hear about psychoanalysis and then to receive these little isolated chapters: number one on instincts, number two on the ego, number three on technique. And, of course, it touched me the way we've just said other concepts touch the whole country. I became a great devotee, because when he said, in a very succinct way, such and such is due to castration anxiety, I didn't need any more proof. I said, "Of course, of course". You just think about it a little bit: That's due to castration anxiety. For example, a guy is having a dream were his hand falls off, and that's due to castration anxiety. I didn't need any more convincing of that. I don't know about you. And that to me was psychoanalysis: Fenichel - and I devoured him. And then I went to the army, I left the residency. A little bit of practice. I can give you so much data in two seconds, because it's pouring out of me like a zit.

Please, that's the point.

I once gave it to the author of the Masud Khan book, Linda Hopkins. She wrote in her book that when Leo Rangell started to tell her about Masud Khan, and LA, "I thought he was going to have a heart attack", that's what she wrote in her book. I saw that, and I thought, she's right. I mean I was so worked up about the whole thing every time I'd tell it, I'd get worked up again. Beth [Kalish], my lady friend, had to stop me sometimes. She said she didn't know all this, she lived in this city and she didn't know all this, because most people didn't know it because history covers over.

My father came here, to this country, and my father's sister couldn't get in because of trachoma, and she went to Buenos Aires. And when I went to Buenos Aires for the first time, in the sixties, there was a whole tree coming from my father's sibling living there. And they had me over for Friday night dinner, Shabbat, the whole works and they lived in the middle class, lower middle class.

They were just like my people in Brooklyn, I thought about my aunt and uncle that lived in Brooklyn.

Yes, that's the same with my relatives in the United States, I am the Argentinian for them [laughs].

But you have some New York people?

Yes, I have some New York people.

That was my family, then they settled in Brooklyn and I was born in Brooklyn.

But my American family, some live in Kentucky where there's the Derby, and some other Lemlijs live in Miami.

Beth [Kalish] comes from Nashville, Tennessee. Some Jews went south, they were a little richer and they could travel a little bit, the others just plonked right down, from Ellis Island. They come on a boat and get off the boat. They got a pushcart, started to sell clothing, they were New Yorkers. That's where my father met my mother who was a seamstress in a seamstress factory, the kind that burned down at one time.

The one that led to the big strike in 1909.

So, you are the Argentinian branch, while I am the American New York branch. Beth is [from the] Southern Jewish branch. A whole different generation, she's 20 years younger than me. You are probably her age, she's 77. You are younger...

A little younger, I am 72.

Harold Blum is my next generation. In a meeting, when I introduced him, I said to the audience that "one generation is handing the baton over to another", and I handed it over to him, because he was coming in, as editor of the journal, and I was going out as president of the American. And we met, and we just took [to] each other like this (*snaps fingers*). But he's like my kid brother, no he's younger, he's like my children. My daughter's age is 69 or 70. I have a son-in-law who just had an 80th birthday, my son-in-law in Hawaii, I just was there where it was celebrated.

You were talking about the misnomer of "ego psychology".

In 1939 Freud died. That same year Heinz Hartmann appeared with *Ego Psychology and the Problem of Adaptation*. That's the second bible after *The Interpretation of Dreams*. When Hartmann died, I gave a memorial. I was president of the International Psychoanalytical Association (IPA) and I said that Freud had reached a mountain top in 1939. It's like he had extracted everything that can be extracted from the id interpretations of the dreams and the early papers in the '20s and he handed the baton to Heinz Hartmann who moved over and carried it to the next mountain, which was the ego. Now Joseph Sandler thinks he invented the superego because of safety. Everyone wrote a few good papers. Sandler's great paper was on the feeling of safety as the counterpart to the feeling of anxiety. I think Freud's first best book was *The Interpretation of Dreams* and that *The Problem of Anxiety* was his second-best book because anxiety runs through all of human history and all through medicine, surgery, podiatry, chiropractic, you name it. Buddhism, yoga, it's all how to manage with anxiety and Freud made a science out of understanding anxiety. I wrote many good papers on anxiety afterwards.

I wrote about the unitary theory of anxiety in which I fused Freud's two theories of anxiety into one.

Can you explain a little bit because that's a whole other huge subject?

When Freud changed from the first theory of, you remember what it was, *actual neurosis*, and who believed in that? Fenichel. He was a strong believer in the first theory of anxiety. Freud then made a revolutionary concept in 1926, that this wasn't just the body reaction to increased tension of undischarged libido, therefore tension on the brain, tension on the spinal cord, tension on the mental apparatus, and that the inability to contain the hyper-excitation of the first theory, led to a threatened mental breakdown for which defenses were erected to prevent it… he conceived.

Then the second [theory of anxiety], in fact, in 1926 he really entered for the first time the psychological meaning of anxiety instead of the physiological meaning of anxiety. He said that this is a threat, which has a mental accompaniment of breakdown. How many patients come in and say, "I think I am going crazy. I am going crazy. I am not going to be able to take care of myself. I am not going to be able to contain my impulses". So Freud conceived of the idea that anxiety is really a sign of danger. Well, it's not the physiological explanation but the fact that panic ensues. The person experiences the fantasy of breakdown, which is the panic state, which goes from 1 plus to 4 plus. Panic can be mild anxiety. Mild anxiety is not panic, panic is when you get 4 plus anxiety. Max Schur developed that a lot, where anxiety becomes the maximum, and then the patient feels a nervous breakdown. So the whole second theory, the second book on anxiety was to me a brilliant exposition of the way the unconscious acted like the smartest part of the individual, not the primitive, but the most alert, the most lifesaving, because the unconscious sensed the imminent presence of a traumatic state, and therefore erected defenses. The second theory of anxiety became a psychological theory of a fear of danger - anxiety being the danger signal and that became known as the 'signal theory of anxiety'.

Now, after that, the field was in state of confusion for a while, and no one ever thought about this thing before, the same as when he changed from trauma to fantasy and again they didn't know which was which, it was Anna O. and all the early patients, due to the fact that they'd been abused by their bad fathers. Yeah, in 1890 everyone thought that, until he came along and said "Why are we blaming these poor old men for having seduced their daughters? Their daughters wanted it. It was their fantasy and sometimes it didn't even happen". They were telling the analyst that they were seduced because they had a fantasy of being seduced. That is when he told Wilhelm Fliess, I don't know when anymore, "I will leave the whole field." and Fliess said, to stay with it, you know that's important. So right after that, a lot of people felt that Freud had changed from seduction to fantasy, but history shows, and my opinion is, that **he didn't change from seduction to fantasy, he added fantasy to seduction** and I have a mantra called **'add, do not replace'**. When you make a new discovery don't throw out the old, keep the old and the new and you've got both. Now I applied that to the theory of anxiety, no one else did. When he doubted the actual neurosis and came up with the psychological theory of anxiety, two famous subsequent writers Robert Waelder and Charles Brenner, said Freud threw out the first theory and came to the second theory, and anxiety is now the signal of danger, nothing else. Fenichel in his book kept the actual neurosis but didn't know what to do with this signal of anxiety thing - the new one.

I wrote two papers, one was the presidential address, and one was delivered at a joint meeting with the American Psychiatric Association. One was in 1954 and the other in 1968, fourteen years apart. The first one was on the unitary theory on anxiety, in which I said that all the phenomena that Freud described clinically and theoretically up until 1926 in his first edition of what anxiety was... [they] are not to be thrown out but are valid and demonstrable. I can see that in every patient, a fear of been overwhelmed with neurosis. But the actual neurosis sends a signal to the mental apparatus which Freud didn't discover until 1926. So, my idea in the first paper was that the actual neurosis furnished a signal of danger thereby uniting theory one and theory two, and that both were retained. Brenner, who's a little sarcastic compared to Waelder, always took the attitude that only people who are crazy think that Freud retained the first theory. And Waelder just says, as a matter of fact in his book, that Leo Rangell is one of the few people who believes that both theories existed. He didn't mention Fenichel by the way, he just mentioned me. And I read that, and I felt very flattered, I mean I respect Waelder to the sky, and if he thinks that of me even though he disagrees with it, I am going to stand by my guns because I really believe that. So, in 1968, fourteen years later at the presidential address to the American Psychoanalytic Association I gave the second salvo as to why I think the two theories are one and each was the mirror image of the other. It's very interesting, no one has ever studied this in detail. To me it's the prelude to the unitary theory of psychoanalysis. Pluralism? I am not a pluralist. I am a unifier. Cláudio Laks Eizirik is a pluralist, Eizirik said in Chicago "Let's face it, we are now a pluralistic science, one is as good as the other" and he gave the medal for the best scientist to Roy Schafer who switched from Freud to Klein. They gave him the medal. Schafer was not the best scientist in the field at all. He's completely contradictory, as I pointed out in *My Life in Theory*. I have a whole chapter on Schafer, where everything he says contradicts what he said before. He's a bundle of contradictions and Eizirik picked him for scientist of the year. You can see that bothered Blum and me. Blum told me privately that he thinks that Eizirik gave him that prize to give him a reward for becoming a Kleinian.

Do you think it was a prize, just a consolation prize?

A reward, yeah, a bribe in a way, and a prize. He became a Kleinian because he married a Kleinian, his second wife was a Kleinian, his first wife was a Freudian, so he was a Freudian.

So, my development is, I first unified the anxiety theory, then I unified psychoanalytic theory and I wrote a book called *The Path to Unity* [Correct title - *The Road to Unity in Psychoanalytic Theory*]. I don't know if you know that book, it's never been taken up. If *the Compromise of Integrity* [full title - *The Mind of Watergate: An Exploration of the Compromise of Integrity*] is stuck in mystique, *The Path to Unity* left them cold, nobody ever reacted to it. I will show it to you inside.

Why do you say that it was not accepted?

Because everybody defends his territory and when your territory is Bion, it's Bionian, when it's Klein, it's Kleinian. When it's Stolorow, it's Stolorowian, when it's Harry Stack Sullivan, it's Sullivanian. When it's Melanie Klein, it's Kleinian, and so on. To me, I have my genealogy that I trust forever. I don't raise them and drop them. My genealogy, which I clearly state in *My Life in Theory*, is Freud. I mean my theoretical genealogy, not my blood genealogy or my analyst - didn't expect my analyst to do much - they didn't do anything much. These guys were not my analysts, they were all people I read and agreed with. My analyst, I never idealized, I had three different analysts. I would never mention one of them in my books. They didn't write anything, they didn't impress me, they didn't even strike me as being particularly honest or conventional or consistent. They were OK in different ways but coming back, my genealogy was Sigmund Freud, Anna Freud, Fenichel, Hartmann, Rapaport. Then, coming into the next generations Leo Stone, then Jacob Arlow and Brenner who were close to me but at the end we had a little trouble.

With Brenner?

While they were alive - they are both gone now - we were a trio Jacob Arlow, Brenner, Rangell. I went along partly because I went along, like everyone goes along. When Arlow and Brenner wrote their book on topography called *A Structural View* [full title - *Psychoanalytic Concepts and the Structural Theory*] saying that the structural view replaced the topographic point of view, I never said, "No" until they died, later. And in many writings, in recent years, I said that I didn't believe that for one minute.

Why didn't you...?

Because again 'add, not replace', the structural view was added to the topographic view. What reason is there to give up the topographic view? Isn't the differentiation between conscious, preconscious and unconscious very important? Why give it up? For streamlining? Why? You are not designing a train, trying to streamline it! You are trying to keep the mental apparatus of the human being, which is multi-layered and diverse. By the way, the unitary theory is very diverse; it puts all the parts together. Bion has a place in my theory, I don't have a place in his, but he has a place in mine... And Kohut, I have a whole story with Kohut. Just the day that he lost the election to me, he became a Kohutian.

Do you think it was a political consequence? Theory following politics...

I proved it. I can quote it word for word. I always say, "Heinz Kohut became a Kohutian on July the so and so, at 11 a.m. in Rome". We were both at the platform and he turned to me and he said, "I don't know how you could want to be president, God, I never would've wanted to be president. I am not a politician, I am a scientist". And I swallowed that because I didn't believe it, but I kept the peace. Afterwards his correspondence came out, books, in which he wrote to Anna Freud that he wrote a hundred letters around Europe trying to get people to support him for the presidency, and to me he'd said on the platform "How could you want to be president?" And many years later, when Robert Wallerstein became president, he wrote to him a letter of congratulations, and he said to him "congratulations on being president, I am sure you will do a very good job. Of course, we all choose to do what we want to do. You should be the president if that's what you want to do, but I could've been president, but I didn't want it so therefore I gave it up in favor of the theoretical development of self-psychology". Bullshit! Anna Freud backed him completely. Why? Because Greenson was her pal and she heard that Greenson and I were like this and she asked Greenson "What's the trouble between you and Leo Rangell?" And he wrote a letter to her, which was a complete lie as to what the trouble really was. And I've got that letter which he wrote to her and it's going to go to the Library of Congress. He said that it all started in the army, and some cockamamie thing that he made up, which I proved was a falsehood. He lived in a different city at the time, it's just a complete rationalization… He didn't want to say what the real thing was, that we disagreed and we had different characters from beginning to end.

Was it a matter of character?

Character, and honesty, and charisma. He [Greenson] was a charismatic, so was Masud Khan; Anna Freud was not so charismatic. Heinz Kohut was not so charismatic except in some very subtle way. He's got very devoted followers but they write. I mean the literature on Kohut, that since then I followed closely. They all started to speculate, When did he become a Kohutian? because he was a complete Freudian up to a certain point. And they give different reasons for it, all of which are completely indefensible. And they never, never, referred to what I said in *My Life in Theory*.

Our field has never followed logic even in explaining the development of our own theory. You asked me, "Why did Bion not meet me here?" Bion knew who I was. I was not at his feet, [not at] Melanie Klein's feet. People sat on the floor under her skirt. It was one evening that I was invited to meet Melanie Klein in London, during my first trip to Europe, which was in 1959. She was sitting in the middle of the room in a chair and all of her disciples were sitting on chairs, but some of them on the floor. She had a big dress like this and they were sitting around her. I thought it was as funny as could be.

That is not something that happens in the United States, I mean that sort of idealizing?

Also. In fact, she was the first dissident, really, after Jung and those people…

What did you think when seeing this scene of the disciples just adoring her?

Well, I used to hear what the Kleinians said and it made me laugh. It was a joke. It was a joke. It was humor. It wasn't factual. The baby wanted to devour the breast and spit it out, or shit it out. I listened to those stories. I thought they were interesting. I was seeing patients already. I never saw anything like that.

There's a funny story about Bion that will take too long to tell. This guy Brandchaft was an activist - a former communist, even in the political front he was very, very left wing, as I was too but [I was] not quite [as much as he was]. He was a friend of my younger brother who was very communist. He got kicked out of school for being on a podium screaming about Earl Browder, the head of the Communist party for many years, like Norman Thomas of the Socialist party. Brandchaft became a doctor in my footsteps because he met me when I was a doctor. So, he followed me. He was a few years behind me. [Then] came the war and this great idealist escapes army service by going to an Indian reservation in Utah. There he calls up Leo Rangell, who's now becoming known in a place called Los Angeles and it was very appealing to him to come to LA, as it was to me and everybody. LA is the playground of America, it's a great place here in many ways. He came here and he immediately, as nobody came from an Indian reservation, got invited. I got him his first analyst. He took an office in my building, he moved in my neighborhood. He came to my house and borrowed my dishes, started to make parties for everybody borrowing from here. And when I became president of the APsaA, well that was like 'wow', and he was sort of a nobody at that time. I remember having invited him to this room to do teaching. We had a seminar here, we were sitting around here, and I, as a young teacher, was teaching the basic drives of sex and aggression. He would come to the meeting with a cigar, smoking a cigar when no one else smoked, came late, interrupting everyone. I was introducing him to the society. He sat there and then he said, "I don't know about sex and aggression, I think it's all aggression and no sex." So he took a polarized position, he separated sex and aggression. I would be for sex, he would be for aggression, his own territory, which was insane.

When I became the president of the American, I started to move up in the international. He made his first trip to Europe, he interviewed Hanna Segal, and he privately invited her to come to Los Angeles to do supervisions outside the institute, which he was now a student of. So there was a Kleinian period. Everyone was dazzled by Klein then, like they were later by Betty Joseph. She took Hanna Segal's place. After the honeymoon was over with Hanna Segal, Brandchaft found Bion and he brought him over here. And I remember the first meeting where he introduced Bion to the society as a tank commander in the British Army. I remember sitting in the audience, and thinking, "that qualifies him to be quite the analyst, a tank commander in the British Army, it qualifies him to get in the front with a gun, yeah, but where does it come to this." So, I am in the audience, and Brandchaft, who was somebody up there, introduces Bion and he comes out at one side of the stage and he walks to the center of the stage and he turns around and he's as imposing as can be, charismatic. He starts to talk and says: "I will give you a case example… the patient… says… to me…. I hate you… I… looked at her… and I said… Oh!" And at this point Leo Rangell gets up from the audience and walks out of the room. Everyone saw me, the whole audience saw me walk out, but this was enough for me, I couldn't take it anymore. Five minutes later Adam Limentani calls me from London "I hear you walked out on Wilfred." "How do you know?" "Well the people told me immediately, that you walked out on Wilfred Bion." I said, "Did you know what he said?" No, he didn't know. Like he liked Kohut, he liked Bion. Adam was a peacemaker, a great guy, a really good friend of mine. Anyway, that was me on Bion, and

Bion was not a friend of mine and he never had an occasion to meet me, nor did I think he was against me, he just probably didn't feel I was really friendly to him.

Or agree with your views.

Of course not! No. But I never would have gone for soup. I wouldn't have wanted to have a heart-to-heart with him. It wasn't in me to start arguing with the whole world. I was arguing with everybody, about anxiety, about unification. I needed to take that on. Yet that [what Bion said] was just too crazy for words. I would say sometimes to the students that, "According to one of these deviant schools of thought you enter each hour without having memory, desire or understanding." I said it has aroused a great deal of approval and sympathy.

Why?

So, I said, "I tried to put it on for size" but first of all I said, "Freud said do not have too much therapeutic zeal". That I agree with, don't come in with therapeutic zeal, be neutral and ready for surprises, and I said I agreed completely. I avoid too much zeal. I try to be neutral and I am always ready for what the patient says, not what I say. But I said "memory, desire and understanding", that's it.

So that was the deal, we never had a clash of any kind, but he'd be surprised to hear all of this. But you are asking me so I am telling you what was at this end. Bion had an illness and he wanted to die in London. Literally, the tank commander wanted to die with his troops, so he went back home. Now, it's not important because of Bion, he himself might've been a wonderful analyst and smart and wrote a couple of good papers on the working group. And the idea of not being seduced at any particular hour is a good idea too, but the school of Bionism is nuts, it's crazy. There's a South

American who was a Bionian. She was Horacio Etchegoyen's secretary at the IPA [Ana Maria Andrade de Azevedo].

Ana María Andrade from Sao Paulo, where they have a Bionian touch.

Seriously, they write a lot about Bion. I have a lot of books here about Bion…

But look, also in Los Angeles…

Now, what I was describing to you, the whole time was an acting-out that led to a window in Los Angeles for European dissidents. Whoever they are, it started with Melanie Klein, went on to Bion, then to Winnicott, they loved Winnicott too. All the people who were on the fringe there, but not Anna Freud; and Ralph Greenson was a hypocrite. Greenson had a close relationship with Anna Freud and was also pals-ing up [getting close] with Brandchaft and Hanna Segal. He went to the seminars that she was giving here. And there's another thing, me and André Green had a big debate at one time about them. It was during a Congress in London in 1975.

I was at that Congress.

Well, that was a very ugly thing where I suffered great pain by the French Nation. They hated me because I defeated Green theoretically. He had nothing to say. I thought we were having a debate on changes in technique, and I was saying again ('add, not replace') that there hadn't been great changes. And he was saying that the advent of a new type of patient today leads to a new type of psychoanalysis. And so, I went down on the things I disagreed with him, and he had no comeback to what I said, and afterwards the people, the French in the audience, wouldn't talk to me, they were so mad at me. Andre Green himself. So Eizirik gave Green the next IPA medal, after Schafer.

But what happened?

I have the tapes of those things, which would be great to listen to again because Green thinks that I was cruel to him. He's very sort of wary of me now, when he meets me he's sort of nice, but once said publicly "I won't do to you what Leo Rangell did to me in 1975". And I didn't do anything to him except refute what he said and give him better arguments. In New York, Woody Allen's analyst, in his pictures, this Viennese guy who wrote about dissidence, he wrote a book on dissident theories. Recently I had a little debate with William Meissner. He just died. They asked me to comment on his paper on unconscious evolution. That's one of my pet subjects. Unconscious decision making, secondary process in the ego. You asked about ego psychology. Id psychology can have secondary process the way ego psychology does. Martin Bergmann wrote one of the great debates in psychoanalysis comparable to the British discussions.

The controversial discussions in 1941-1945.

The next important debate was between André Green and Leo Rangell. And he says, "Anna Freud supported Leo Rangell and those two won the debate hands down, but posterity showed that Green was the real winner because Green was for pluralism at that time, and everyone went his way". By the way, Anna Freud was no great ally, she was very reluctant to agree to what I was saying. I had a lot of trouble in private correspondence with Anna Freud on which I write about in *My Life in Theory*. I am so open that I have a minority of people who've read very carefully what I wrote there, including a discussion group in London. I can't think of the names but there are some people who have dissected that book and had a discussion on it in which they admired and thanked me for my candor on what I said about Anna Freud and Masud Khan and people like that. So anyway, ironically, I beat André Green theoretically but politically he won over me.

You think it is so?

Yes, absolutely. I think my view is such a minority today it's almost non-existent, it's only in individuals. For example, Harold Blum. I don't have something like the Kohutian followers. Kohut has a school behind him. You've never heard of a Rangell school of unified theory and unconscious volition.

We were talking about charismatic characters that have particular assets in our psychoanalytic world. Sounds as if you have a strong view on charisma and charismatic leaders.

Yes, well when I stop to think about why that is, it's partly due to principles and theoretical considerations, partly it's due to personal experiences. From the theory point of view my attraction to psychoanalysis, and I think that of Freud, was an attraction to ideas not to people nor concepts. Everyone treasured admirable conceptual thinking, where you could figure things out. That is, after all, a goal of living - to be able to master, to figure out the causes and effects and you become the master. So, autonomy was always a very positive word to me, you analyze someone, and you try to inculcate what we call 'ego autonomy'. That means that he's the master of his own fate, he doesn't depend on suggestion. That [suggestion] was the copper rather than the gold of psychoanalysis, it was suggestion, you are only doing something because another individual is telling you to do it and you want that person to love you, so you take on what he says and do what he wants. But the real advance in maturity and independence is to have 'ego autonomy' or the ability to think for yourself. That to me is inimitable, and [the opposite] then [is] leaning on a person's charming personality. That's really the essence of a good marriage too, to be married because of love, of ways of thinking, of character traits, not ability to seduce. So unfortunately, charisma and the ability to seduce become closely interwoven, a charismatic person is a seductive person. We don't want - I am thinking out loud - an individual to be brought up, either in life or in analysis, to be seducible so that's something you teach your patient to be wary of, to resist, to develop the ability to stand up on his own. That's why Margaret Mahler had such an effect on the field. I met Margaret Mahler when she was young. Yeah, I know all of these people personally, and everything came from personal knowledge. She started to investigate separation-individuation, the opposite of charismatic dependence. She chronicled that when a child, at age 3 says, "No", it's because "I want to do such and such not because Mommy wants me to do it." "Well, I think this is good because, I think it's good, not because my sister or my brother tell me it's good or bad." But that is a milestone in development, all that on the theoretical front. On the interpersonal front as I grew up in psychoanalysis, I saw that the opposite was in truth very rampant, that people followed the leader, like lemmings following the leader into the sea.

I started to hear of Karen Horney when I was young. She was one of the first dissident theorists. It was not Klein but Horney, because of the war coming on. And Harry Stack Sullivan. It was a question of social psychology versus intra-personal psychology. And I always leaned away from following, whether it was the ideology of Marx, or of Sullivan, or of Horney, and instead I gravitated towards a psychology, which centered on making the mind of an individual independent. And that made a stance against charisma, to which I was drawn myself when I first met this Ralph Greenson. I knew him in the army, he was dazzling, the whole post, army post, listened to him while he talked about the psychology of the soldier. We were together in Colorado at the time and I was one of his closest listeners. I was so impressed by how he put his messages across so 'livingly', but he did it, I learned later, by dropping names of his patients, Hollywood patients, fostering rivalries between people. Those that he liked were "okay," those that he didn't, were "no good." He would humiliate people, as well as praise people, and people then sought to be in his favor. And I saw that people like him were divisive in a group, or a post, or an organization, rather than unificatory, the way I was. I mean, I always spoke in common-sense terms, trying, but maybe not being able to be as impressive as he was, but by the same time, my message,

I would think would be more enduring and lasting than ephemeral and opportunistic.

But you are putting charisma together with opportunism - to being an opportunist…

It's close to… It's close to opportunism in that, I think a charismatic person who's not consistent in ways of thinking and theories is most likely to shift from one to the other, the criterion being, which can influence the most people, not which is correct. With Freud it was always the challenge, how do you know what he's saying, how do you put it to the test, that was both his up and his down. It helped him along, but it always made things difficult because the kind of data that he was dealing with were very hard to put to test. You can't treat ten people one way and ten people another way, or a thousand people, and when you do what you do with individuals, it's not as impressive to other individuals, as people who can sway a crowd, a crowd pleaser. Ultimately a Hitler, who can sway not just a crowd but a nation, not just a nation but a world, he had everyone all over the world doing Heil Hitler, if that isn't long enough and deeply enough…

When did you realize that Greenson was not okay? How did it come to you that he was charismatic and not really serious?

I described it in my memoir. I like the word memoir rather than autobiography because it's a reflection of my whole life inside me and outside me. I noticed it looking back, say 30 years later, in the 80's or the 90's. It took many decades to write that book, I noticed in retrospect that we had had a period in the army in Colorado, after I knew Greenson only one year, when the post was divided and there was as much tension between people as there were later in the LA psychoanalytic [society] in the 1960's when it was just a question between who were Greenson's friends and who were his enemies. And those who were friends got patients, and those who quibbled or argued with him too much were out and never got any referrals. But in the army post it was who appeared as a 'smarty' under him, who knew the right gifts, of what to say, or how to make a quip, or funny joke, or put somebody down, take the right positions, and not be ridiculed. Those were the successful ones, so I began to notice, analysts both observe and think. First, they observe and then they think about what they observe, and they try to make sense of it. So the observation I was making was, only the six month development, the one year development of an army group and how it was decimated and fractured and made into two groups, or more, according to where they stood with the charismatic leader and gradually things began to sour, where at first it was all excitement, and the excitement was based on demagoguery. Adhesion to a demagogue, no one knew the word then: 'demagogue'. He was a charmer not a 'demagogue'. So, I became aware of charming people and to be wary of them. And I've always admired more, to this day, the quiet scholarly type than the quick flash of genius.

And what happened here in LA?

Well, I described that the same thing that happened in the army post developed here. Greenson was the most exciting training analyst, public speaker, personal analyst of important people—celebrity analyst. We were all being focused on one person and his little coterie and anyone who agreed with him, and everyone who wasn't part of his parlor game was not invited to his Sunday mornings at home, where they played music sometimes, a lot. You could enjoy the benefits that came with being friends with the star, where you got the friends of the friends of the stars. Everyone was vying for big patients, big practice, nice ways to live, important people to know, popular things to do. Popularity was more important than the steady output of scientific papers, which is what I elected to do, and at first it was not always bad, neither bad nor good. It did a lot of good for me to be putting out all those papers, but it was slow going, it was more a steady improvement in knowledge and technique and popularity—being known by people than it is when you do things dramatically. And then certain things happened, I mean, specific events, there's a thing called "The Wexler Incident" where a patient complained that her analyst, Wexler, had struck her, and I happened to be president [of the Society] at that time, and the complaint came to me and I had the responsibility of doing something about it and a terrible, a terrible group event took place after that. Wexler accused me of harassing him, and he was a lawyer who became an analyst, and he said that my administration was harassing him and not proceeding according to due process of law and he suggested that I should be investigated for what I was doing rather than he be investigated for what the patient was complaining about, which is what happened. A committee was set up and they began to look into the matter of how we went about dealing with the complaint of the patient and it led to another great divisiveness among the membership of the society, which eventually led to a split society, and to the invitation to the British Kleinians to come into LA. To me, the two were related although it's never been actually proven or shown on paper or presented to the public as such, but it appears in a lot of my writings.

So, they invited the British Kleinians to come here.

Privately.

What were the effects of that?

The effect was that it split the LA Society into Freudians and Kleinians. And the Kleinians became derisive of the Freudians, and disdainful with them, and the Freudians became either defensive, very much like in Britain. The Anna Freud group was the third out of the three: Klein, object relations, and Freud.

The Freudians were not the leaders, they were the defenders.

Why? The same as here?

The same as here, new territory is always more welcome than old territory… conquer the West, territorial expansion.

Perhaps also I am thinking that Kleinian ideas are more attractive to charismatic people.

And to their followers, they are more easily followed, they are more dictatorial, they are more 'conflictful'. We just say that 'It is so', I told you before about a child having all these bizarre fantasies about eating and devouring, that's never put into words. It's always what we now call projective identification on the part of the analyst. He projects those things onto the patient, the patients don't tell him about what they thought when they were six months old, no patient ever told me that, ever. I never ever observed it, so I have to take someone's word for it? But I'd rather believe what the patient told me claiming that he was having a dream that was suggesting to me castration, like I told you before, rather than he wanted to eat up the nipple.

Have you not been intrigued by the fact that so many people actually take to those ideas?

I surely have. The whole South American continent for example, why are they so Kleinian in unison, and the Americans, not in unison, on ego psychology? Are the Americans more practical? Are they more realistic? Are they more 'show me' types? You have to show me before I believe it. To all extent, to some extent. All of those things…

Yes, but Kleinianism is losing strength in Latin America, I think Winnicott is in a way taking over.

How do you explain it?

My idea is that Kleinians and Winnicottians have something in common, simple ideas that serve as a locomotive to add any wagons you want. So, in a way, you talk about projective identification, you know the Kleinian ideas, and it's a cliché that you can use for everything.

Right.

And I think about Winnicott and I have strong disagreements with some of my good friends there, because Saul Peña and Max Hernández are very Winnicottian. It's a transitional object and transitional space, and you use that cliché for everything you want. So that's my idea, I don't know how you feel. So, it's a simple "psychoanalytic" quote-unquote concept and you can use it for absolutely everything.

Correct, and after Winnicott it's something else, Bion. I mean Bion's idea is...

But there's a difference, I think Bion is more mystique. It has a more religious touch, or his followers see him as a messiah, which is not the case, I think, with Winnicott. A bit with Klein. But that means that in fact analysts don't like to think that much now.

Why is Freudianism the last of the three? There always has to be someone else, why doesn't it satisfy them to stick with the observable Oedipus complex at age 5. That's not mystique, that's observed in children. Everyone observes it in their own children, in himself, and in his own patients. So why is it they are so defensive and easy to be shaken away from it?

You tell me...I can give you some information about Latin America. I reviewed the bibliography of twenty years of papers in Latin America. The most quoted author, nearly a thousand quotes in the twenty years, was Winnicott. About nine hundred odd quotes, the second was Melanie Klein about a hundred less. So, Winnicott is more quoted now than

Melanie Klein, and I only found nine quotes related to Anna Freud. So, Anna Freud is nearly not used, taken for granted, yes, but not quoted in Latin America. But she's quoted in psychiatric papers, not in psychoanalytic ones.

Where am I quoted? No place.

Yes, but I think the most known work of yours….

Is "Integrity"…

Is "Integrity", not your psychoanalytic papers. But I suppose that it's the truth about most North American authors, except Otto Kernberg. Which is odd because Otto, of course, is Latin American himself and has toured quite a lot and he was president of the IPA in recent years.

And he's always quoting the others. Melanie Klein and Bion, he dips into all of them and that gives him some credibility.

And somebody who's being quoted a lot now is Peter Fonagy.

He's the latest craze, he took Sandler's place, Sandler appointed Fonagy as his successor.

You were going to tell me something about Sandler.

When I was president of the IPA, until that moment and for some time later, the election was always the election of president. And after the president was elected he named his secretary, and nobody knew who the secretary was until the president was selected. It was always the person running on his name recognition whether he was known or not, and I was perfectly ready to do that, and I won on that. I won against two very difficult opponents: Arlow and Kohut. I never would have predicted that I would be the winner. Kohut said he didn't want it, but he wrote hundreds of letters for it, and Arlow was also interested, but before he died he told Blum that he never wanted it. That was not true, I know it wasn't true, but I won it because Great Britain favored me, for some reason. They'd never met me but Adam Limentani told me the first time he met me, he said "You are going to be the next president", I said "Why do you say that?", he said "Because our society had a caucus and they decided that they wanted you of the three, and I am sure that's going to happen", and then it happened. Several elections later Sandler is running, only the presidents were known [in the election, not the secretary], it was neck and neck, but no one knew who was going to win. The meeting where they did the counting [of the votes] was the business meeting in Rome.

The person who's elected is one of the ones who is sitting in that room, not by mail ballot. If people were out vacationing in Rome then they lost their votes, everyone knew who was going to vote for whom. A few days before the election Sandler announced publicly that his choice for secretary was Jacqueline Amati Mehler, and then he won the election. Amati Mehler was a Roman, the whole room was filled with Italians, that was enough to put him way over the hill. From then on, every president names his secretary in advance and this person is the one who's calculated to bring him votes from an area that's weak. Sandler started that, nobody ever picked that up, and said "Why did he do that?". He didn't do it because Amati Mehler was his choice, he did it because that was the way to get elected that day, that's the story.

Horacio Etchegoyen was the last elected in a general meeting, from then on it was ballots, correspondence. What do you think about this change?

It made it more democratic. It would prevent what just happened, what I just told you. Were you aware of that?

Well, not exactly like that but I remember very well the election. I was in Rome and I remember Joe Sandler and Jacqui Amati being elected...

But did you ever put cause and effect together?

No, not really.

Think about it for a minute.

I think, you put as secretary somebody who can give you votes.

It started with Sandler, before that people didn't do that. I didn't name anyone who I knew would get me votes. I didn't even know who was going to be my secretary until after I was elected. I did not make the choice. I didn't think of who I would name because I didn't think I was going to be elected. After I was elected I had a minute to think about, "Now who's secretary?"

You think it was better?

More honest, it was more honest, yeah.

Because you could choose the best person for the job.

Absolutely, for the job, it had nothing to do with the election anymore, it was after, an afterthought. People didn't even know about it. They went home not knowing who the secretary was.

Now you were saying that you ran against Arlow and Kohut. Both denied that they wanted to be elected. You think it was so shameful to be defeated?

They didn't want to be defeated, not shameful but they didn't like it. They didn't say that before the election, they said it afterwards. Never before, no. Before they would've withdrawn, they didn't withdraw, neither withdrew.

Yes, but you said that in a way, Kohut changed his psychoanalytic thinking.

He was writing *The Analysis of the Self*. It was pro Anna Freud at that stage, so much so that he also wrote in his correspondence that he had certain conferences in his mind all planned, conferences on ego psychology, structural psychology, and the chairman of them would be Seymour Lustman, someone whom Anna Freud would love.

Lustman is from Yale and was a pal of Albert Solnit who was a pal of Anna Freud, and there was even talk of Lustman becoming Anna Freud's successor at the Hampstead Clinic. So, Kohut told Anna Freud that he's got it all planned, "We are going to have training conferences and the chairman will be Seymour Lustman." And then what happened? Seymour Lustman drowned in the Atlantic Ocean in a boat, a fishing boat, he died. And the whole thing was changed, but then Kohut becomes a self-psychologist, some people think he didn't even take the unconscious into account anymore, let alone the structural view. He was all about the cohesion of the self. The cohesion of the self was pre-analytic; you didn't need to have psychoanalysis to have total self-regard or self-protection. It's only when you broke it down into the structures of the mind that you began to think of the true psychoanalytic goals in the analytic process, the ego mastering, the input from the id, and the super ego, and the external world, following Anna Freud's equidistant position that she wrote about in 1936, *The Ego and the Mechanisms of Defense*. Joe Sandler was completely with her while she was alive and only switched to the middle school of London after Anna Freud died.

Do you think that it was just political convenience?

A hundred percent, what else was there? Did he have a change of heart? Theoretically?

But you have mentioned several people doing that… It seems there are not analysts with strong convictions.

I say that, yes. That wouldn't have been true with everybody, wasn't true with me, it wasn't true with Solnit, it wasn't true of Lustman, wasn't true of Arlow, of Brenner. They didn't become Kleinians but they became diluters of Freud a little bit.

Why did they dilute it or put a bit of water in the wine? Or a bit of copper in the gold? Or what? You say that in a way they left a bit of Freud and became something else?

Yes, by picking up the structural view. Brenner did it at the end of his life, Arlow and Brenner did it in the monograph on the topographic view. At the end of Charlie's life, he reneged on the whole meta-psychology.

You were mentioning also the way Roy Schafer changed his views. The question is about change. You were mentioning changes that are okay, and changes that are not.

I have given you examples of people that had a sudden unexpected change of course from north to south, from east to west, not due to new data, and therefore scientifically motivated like Freud when he changed from seduction to trauma… [or] rather from seduction to fantasy, on the basis of new observations. Over the course of a psychoanalytical lifetime I have noticed a tremendous gradual evolutionary change in what I see, in what I do, in what I think are the goals of psychoanalysis and the methods of psychoanalysis. I was thinking there was a big change in analysis, when analysts moved from a professional medical building to practice in their homes where patients began to see their pictures on the walls and how they lived and guessed who their family was. That already introduced a certain subjectivity to what we considered what was a neutral position, but it was never really completely neutral, there was always the clothes we wore, the culture we come from, how we talked and what our values were. Well, I maintained that in my development, for 70 years as an analyst, I went on steadily like any good Freudian should. I believe I changed with the times realistically. Analysis changed from 6 times a week to 5 times a week, to 4 times a week, to 3 times a week. And we keep arguing, what's the bottom line, we have become much more human beings in our analysis.

I think at the beginning everyone strove to be an automaton and a machine and a reflex inanimate object that the patient would react to. The concept of the silent analyst or the blank screen, was open to ridicule. It was very hard for a person to become blank. Everyone has expressions on his face. You can't be a blank. But I think that as time went on I, like every other analyst, one generation after the other, relaxed and changed in a beneficial and less constricted way. So, one day I moved from my office in Beverly Hills to my office at home, where you sit now. This is a completely different environment than I had there, it was more like going into a laboratory, it was more like having a blood test, rather than being talked to. And yet everyone was talking about inner lives, but when I came home, and they were coming here, saw my garden and my ambiance and maybe saw a kid running around now and then, there was progression in treatment. There's such a mingling of the personal and the professional that one has to know where the line is drawn. Well, I think that the analyst grows with such experiences, from one thing to another. I remember I can almost picture that one day I took my tie off and came into the office like this. Before that I had a shirt and tie on every morning, every day. All of us did, in 1940 we had a shirt and tie, in 1950 we came in like this, in 1960 I had a cup of coffee with me. Everything was for a more relaxed analyst, never a less.

I tried to maintain boundaries in treatment where we had difficulty maintaining boundaries. So again the goal was 'add, do not replace', add humanity without removing objectivity, but don't add humanity like Franz Alexander did, with a corrective emotional experience that eliminated the neutral position that Fenichel was advocating. I was after a blend of the two, to be human and objective at the same time, and you could tell by how a patient talks, how an analyst talks to his patient when his attitude is to the outside world, towards telephone calls, towards outside concerns, and many things, many events happened which I recorded like that, like fire. One day I looked out my window in Beverly Hills and half the city was on fire, in 1963. Four hundred homes were being burned within sight of where I was sitting. You can't maintain a neutral attitude towards the patient in front of you, you wonder where are both your houses at the time. So, with that in mind I considered this: Arnold Richards says that he and Brenner and the New York vanguard group became 'modern conflict theorists.' I asked him, "What is a 'modern conflict theorist'?" "Well it's different from an old Freudian theorist." "How?" "He has different concepts of conflict." "What's the difference? The Freudian concept was ego vs. id, what's the modern conflict theorist? What is modern conflict theory today? Kernberg? What does Kernberg depend on as far as conflict is concerned?" That links it to conflict between object and self-representations in the ego. The conflict is between the identified self and object within the ego, no longer between the ego and the id. If you stop to think of that and spend a day with students, mulling that over, it's a complete change in the meaning of psychoanalysis. If there's no longer a defense against impulses from within, instinctual drives, if you give up drives as substitute object representations, you are a different analyst than I am.

But you are saying that in a way, Arnold Richards and Otto Kernberg share that?

Arnold is wishy washy about it because I've had arguments with him and he always says that he believes what I believe. But then when he writes he writes something else, he writes about 'modern conflict theory'. So I say I am not the same kind of modern theorist as you are, he said "Well, what are you?" **I am a developed Freudian who retained Freudianism and added very strongly the pre-oedipal of Klein, object relations of Fairbairn, transitional object from Winnicott, they all belong on my tree but so does the trunk.** I don't alter or discard the trunk. And when I told you that I had a little difficulty at the end with both Arlow and Brenner, both of whom were very dear friends of mine at different times, it's because I really, really didn't believe that the structural view eliminated the topographic or economic view. There's a book co-written by Anna Freud and Joseph Sandler, reminiscing about Anna Freud's 1936 book *The Ego and the Mechanisms of Defense* in which Anna Freud says what I am saying now, that the topographic and economic points of view, which the New York group tried to do without, in her view, was still existent and very important, which I agree with, which Sandler in talking to Anna Freud, agreed with. Sandler and Wallerstein ran the Anna Freud symposia before she died, the last few years, every year, every other year. There was a symposium in the London area.

Joseph Sandler was involved in one of those, on identity and the analyst. He wrote a book about it. So those two people were thorough Anna Freudians in conducting those weekend meetings. When Anna Freud died in 1983, Sandler's next book was on projective identification, which he had opposed while Anna Freud was alive, because that was a Klenian-Bionian concept. Afterwards, he wrote a book clarifying; a pretty good book, clarifying projective identification and making amends with it, and becoming a darling of the object relations British Middle School. And Wallerstein gave his famous address in 1987 after Anna Freud died on "no one theory supersedes any other, each one is as good as any other". And when I countered that and said that I don't agree, I think the Freudian theory supersedes the others, he was very insulted, he said, I am making sort of a fool out of what he's saying. That's where we had our rift. He wrote a little paper about where he and I agree and disagree, I don't know if you saw it, a very important paper.

How do you see he has evolved because he's known, I think, outside of the United Stated mainly because of that paper "One Theory or Many?".

What did you think his conclusion was about "One Theory or Many?"

Well, that there is one clinical practice, but you can explain it in different ways. That one clinical experience, in a sense, can be explained and the theories might diversify, but actually analysts do the same thing regardless of their theories. I am not sure that this is the case...

Well, you will have to read the correspondence between him and me on that. I felt that he was saying that no theory has a right to claim being superordinate over any other. That's what I extracted, and I say that's not true. I think that Freudian theory has a right to say that it's superordinate to the Kleinian theory, to Harry Stack Sullivan, to Bion, to Kohut, to Fairbairn. I don't think that we have six or seven different, equal theories, with several different trunks. I think the whole tree has one trunk and the branches are infinite in their number, they could go anywhere including way off into the political, psycho-political environment. Economic even, even Wall Street, everywhere: art, literature, music... So that I consider myself a 'developed Freudian'. You know there are colleagues who are writing on Leo Rangell's 'developed Freudian' idea.

What happened to Roy Schafer who has taken in some of the Kleinian ideas?

Roy Schafer's first split was from Rapaport in Topeka. Where he wrote a new language for psychoanalysis, where he cast out on the structural theory, having explanatory value in explaining human action and behaviour, and he wrote a new action theory à la George Klein, not Melanie Klein. George Klein, saying that, it's very similar to Kohut, saying that the self is the agent not the ego. All my writings say that the ego is the agent not the self, the ego acts for the self. The hand that holds a pen or a bullet is not the master, it's the brain, ordering the hand to write this, or to shoot to die with aggression or to marry someone you love. The agent, the executive agent of the human mental apparatus, in my way of thinking, is the human structure ego not the total cohesive self which contains id and superego and external world.

That's why I have that thought out as to what American psychoanalysis really amounted to. It was never ego alone, that was a shortcut, a falsification, misleading, a "misleader". It's all very clear in my mind, it's very, very clear, and I have very few followers that are devoted. I run a private group you may know of, between here and San Francisco, I have a group of about ten, twelve people, we meet regularly, and they all know my point of view which I think more of us share.

So, in a way it's as if American psychoanalysis is misrepresented.

No, they don't misrepresent anything, it's misconceived by the psychoanalytic public. I took this up with a guy named Fred Busch. He's a very strong guy and he's in the IPA's Executive Council as counsellor, he's well-positioned to be elected next time, I think. Anyway, he's somewhat hypocritical in this series, he says he doesn't disagree with me but when he comes into public, he falls into the same trap in order to be popular. He invited me to speak in Boston, he's a Boston guy, and when I made the statement that I am not an ego psychologist, I am an id, ego, super ego, etc., etc., everyone got up, everyone clapped, they applauded, they all agreed. And he got up after me, he was the chairman, and he said, "I am still an ego psychologist". Everyone laughed, I didn't want to say, "Well, then where does the id come in?" I just let it go, because you can't follow it up with these people without getting to the embarrassing, showing them to be crazy or stupid, you can't do that. So, you just do nothing, you let the audience think what they think about this.

But we were talking about the Kleinians with their own small...

So first Roy Schafer was a Rapaportian, that means a Hartmannian, then George Klein led a school away from Rapaport into Merton Gill, Schafer, Holt, Holzman, some of them went to NYU, some of them went to Austen Riggs Center. He then wrote about a new language, which set him off by himself. Then he moved from New Haven to New York and somewhere along the line his wife died. He remarried another wife and she was a Kleinian, and then he wrote a book as an author which was a fusion of Freud and Klein, his version of Kleinianism, and it was opportunistic to be Kleinian in his marriage so he was now joining Ron Britton and all the new London Kleinians. He was going to join the modern Kleinians, so he's the one who coined the words: modern Kleinian and current Freudianism, neo Freudian, I don't know. That they came together, if you modify both, but I found that he was kowtowing the Kleinian ideas and giving up his Freudian metapsychology. The objection that George Klein and that whole school had, was that the Freudian school was mechanistic, and too machine-like, too medical, organ-like. Rather, that it had no soul, had no heart, and the heart of the human being was not the heart of the body but the primitive origins of the human brain, because the later origins became Oedipal, and that's already Freudian so they were stuck with the earliest infantile postnatal life. Some of them then went as far as becoming prenatal life, especially in South America, Arnaldo Rascovsky, the first Rascovsky. He was prenatal, he used to take his analytic candidates out into the woods and have them spread their legs and have their babies with him in the branches watching. He was a jovial, lovable man. He became very close to us, so he once came to visit here, and he was enthralled with Beverly Hills and LA, and he liked my wife Anita a lot. So, my wife Anita took him to Neiman Marcus, the department store, so he would bring home panties and bras for his patients. He would buy them with Anita's supervision.

Was that a joke or…

For real.

Yeah? For real?

It was a joke like Bion was a joke, was it a joke to have no memory, was that a joke or for real?

A metaphor, you think he meant it?

He bought the underwear and he conducted natural childbirth. I don't know that he had that many pregnant patients, but he apparently helped them deliver their babies.

Well, he was a pediatrician originally.

And he believed in prenatal. He also believed that a drug addict was due to the blood, the umbilical cord was insufficient during prenatal life. He believed that.

You were talking about reflectional observation. And on the other hand, we have from Kohut to Rascovsky, different ways of conceptualizing things. Is that analysis? Is that psychoanalysis?

They thought it was.

You don't think so?

No, of course not. Do you think [it is]?

No, I don't think [it is]. But you were talking about adding, what have you obtained or what do you think psychoanalysis has obtained from, say, Kohut?

I can't name one thing in Kohut's self-psychology that's valid and new. Empathy, we don't need Kohut for empathy. Margaret Mahler wrote about the differentiation of self from object and before that there was self-object, then they differentiated to self and object, you can tell which is which. Before that you are fused with the mother. Kohut wrote a whole book about that but that didn't change one thing from what Mahler said thirty years before. She didn't have a separate school, she was part of Freudianism. Phyllis Greenacre was full of insights, there was no school of Phyllis Greenacre, she was all part of Freudianism. Edith Jacobson wrote about the self and the object long before Kohut. What did Kohut add? Phoniness, dogmatisms, the illusion of something new, a cohesive group around which you do a dance.

But why was he so popular? Why did people buy it?

Charisma! Charisma in a negative way with him. He was very dull, Kohut was anything but appealing, like Nixon. And Nixon was very unappealing, he wasn't at all a John F. Kennedy. He was a creepy guy. Kohut was that way too, he was creepy, but he was dogmatic and he frightened people. He frightened his wife and son, I know them both.

But you are saying that to be dogmatic creates a public. You get the clientele out of being dogmatic. You are saying that being dull can be charismatic in a sense.

With a compelling idea, if the compelling idea is empathy. Mother love, mother failure.

But the same thing is with Winnicott, in a sense.

Yes, they are very much overlapping transitionally. Winnicott's holding operation is very much like Kohut's empathy. And someone here is trying to unite Lacan with Kohut and Winnicott as being exactly the same.
   Well I don't understand Lacan's style, what he writes. He's too complicated for me. I find him totally useless.

How about Kohut? Sometimes I use the self-object for teaching purposes.

But what you use, what you say is Kohutian, isn't it Freudian? I use it as part of Margaret Mahler's ideas or Jacobson's. It's Freudian.

Yes. But I think historically, when one talks about American psychoanalysis, Kohut is mentioned.

Right, but did anyone ever say that from Chicago, Kohut went to Rome to become president of the IPA, and then he lost and then he became a Kohutian?

No.

Then he went back to Chicago? That's the facts, they will be disputed, they will be ignored. Do you know John Gedo?

Yes.

Kohut's rival in Chicago in a way. He's got a lot to say about Kohut, he says that Kohut made a homosexual pass at him.

I wonder if that was something similar to you and Greenson here: a split in the psychoanalytic community: Gedo and Kohut.

No, it was long before Kohut, it had nothing to do with Kohut. Greenson didn't know Kohut, Greenson was not as smart as people thought he was. He was charismatic but not brilliant, he didn't write any papers that were startling or sharp, but he was very persuasive. He could have been a movie star. He could have been the hero of any film. They did a film of him in the army, he was Captain Newman. It was about narcosynthesis, which was used by psychoanalysts but now has been totally abandoned.

In Latin America, the best-known work of yours is not the clinical, it's your work on Watergate. It is quite fascinating I suppose because politics is very much something that Latin American psychoanalysts are familiar with.

Do you have the book, the Watergate book?

I have the book, the Spanish version, but I have the English version as well. Saul Peña's translation has become a part of political culture. I wonder if you have developed any ideas about political matters since then.

Yes, a lot, a lot. One thing that interested me before I became an analyst was this. In 1939-1940, I was resident in neurology, psychiatry, psychoanalysis. At that moment my goal was to be a neurosurgeon. At first, I went into the field to study neurology, from neurology I was going to go to neurosurgery. I was not interested in wasting time talking about nebulous things that you can never know anything about. I wanted to see the tumor, take it out, and have the patient better. The stroke is gone, the paralysis is gone, the paraseizures are gone. I was ready to become a surgeon when two things happened. Number one, all the people I was resident with were turning to this new thing called psychoanalysis: Freud, Hartmann, Kris, and Lowenstein invaded New York City. Not Freud, the others, and everyone was talking about psychoanalysis and all the teachers of psychology were psychoanalysts and it became interesting. But more than that, Pearl Harbor broke out and this country was at war, and Hitler was a menace. He was a dangerous poison; a poison was in the air. And I remember having the distinct conflict "Who's best going to be able to serve the world now?" Freud or Marx. Marx had an explanation for it all, class warfare, economic deprivation, and "arise ye soldiers of starvation and ye shall inherit the earth", take it away from the capitalists. The other was Sigmund Freud, who was saying that deep in the hearts of every man he is both good and bad, the evil is in the individual himself. And I remember at that time my brothers and my friends, everyone was left-wing, political left-wing, except those who were going into medicine. Those who were going into medicine were going into nervous system, that was me, I mean, I was nervous system. I remember having the dilemma: should I drop medicine and become a communist or should I drop communism and become a neurologist, psychiatrist, and psychoanalyst? And I remember saying this to myself "Freud can explain Marx, but Marx cannot explain Freud". Freud can explain the neuroticism of the left-wing *politicians*, but the *politicians* have nothing to do with explaining the patients in my neurological hospitals who were having paraseizures and conversions and I was trying to figure out, did they have a spinal cord tumor, or did they have hysteria? And I felt... is Freud and this division of hysteria and organic that's a stamp of the future and we got to get to know Hitler and what the hell is going on in his mind rather than have Karl Marx go in and kill him, or another fascist or communist would come and divide the world. So, I was quite content with my medicine, but I switched from neurosurgery to neuropsychiatry and then psychoanalysis, so I became a psychoanalyst.

When I became a psychoanalyst, in line with what I just told you about, 'add, don't replace', I didn't discard Marxism, I added to it, and I thought that there's plenty of room for capitalist conflict, capitalist socialist conflict. And the biggest psychopathology I came to be seeing after a while was not in my consulting room but in the trenches in France and Germany and what was beginning to happen throughout the world before the concentration camps, that always added spice and it came to be true that the biggest danger in the world was the evil inside of man, the aggressive instinct. I was quite satisfied with my choice, so I became a psychoanalyst, but I didn't lose sight of the political conflicts which were equal to the individual conflicts. Then, to further add to the flames, I left New York in 1943, after my residencies, went to the army and then settled here. The minute I settled here another officer came from the navy, from the South Pacific and settled in Whittier, that's LA. His name was Richard Nixon, he was a congressman, he was a lawyer, but I was a doctor. During my first year here, there was a contest for congressman, and the right-wing republicans around here found this lawyer and trained him to run for congress against the liberal congressman named Jerry Voorhis, he was a very wonderful guy. This unknown guy with a flat nose came on the scene and took papers out of his pocket and he said, "My opponent is a comm-unist, I can prove it he's a comm-unist" as he used to pronounce communist. And he never opened the papers to show why he was a communist, just he'd wave it at the audience, and Richard Nixon became congressman on his first try and it is said that he did not defeat Jerry Voorhis, he killed him, he finished his career. Jerry never showed his face again, he was so ashamed of being called a communist. This guy, Nixon, then went on to become President of the United States, and I was here, and he came from here to Governor of California, to Vice-President under Eisenhower, to President. And I am treating one patient at a time, and I am reading the papers about what this guy, Nixon, is doing and then I read about a burglary at Watergate. I said right away "Nixon's guilty", long before he was proven guilty. And I said that, watching every single day's newspaper predicting the outcome of that Watergate [hearing] and I made notes on it. Later when it came to pass there was the smoking gun, my book was written. I had all the notes, I wrote a book on it, *The Mind of Watergate* and I said there's more to the world than ego, id, conflicts that make neurosis. There are ego-superego conflicts that make for the syndrome of a compromising integrity on a grand scale, on a mass scale, as in Washington DC, in Watergate. Moreover, the important thing is that people would elect a guy like Tricky Dick, without a thought and give him a landslide election, and that's what made the fact that the electorate identifies with the corrupt more than they do with the hysteric or the noble, and that was the book. But then, a country like Peru, which has one corrupt man after another, lapped it up. Every country should have lapped it up. What I am telling you is that my interest in the political periphery of the tree never waned, never disappeared, it was always there. While I was at the trunk I was watching the periphery and when I added that to this, I became who I am now. A classical analyst writing about the electorate of a nation, 300 million people electing Richard Nixon, by a landslide. After the Watergate break in, not before, after they knew he was involved in it, they elected him.

Now, how do you explain that they identify more easily with corruption than with hysteria.

Because we are constantly battling our own impulses to do the same thing, to gain personal advantage over the others. Nixon had no guilt, he did things without guilt, that's what people identified with, they could bring about the oedipal murder and they could not feel guilty about it. Whereas the ordinary person feels guilty about it, but when he votes for a leader who doesn't, he gets a vicarious thrill out of being associated with that leader. He could commit aggression, an aggressive crime, without guilt. Or another example. I have some great examples with Nixon.

Nixon is given credit for going into China. Nobody but him could have gotten into China, he wouldn't have allowed it, he would have called them communists. So, he was the first to go in and someone wrote that it was like giving a medal to [the one] who starts a fire and then calls a fire engine to put it out. Every person has a fantasy that you rob a bank and then you get a medal for exposing someone that has robbed a bank, which you did. I showed that there are different mechanisms to talk about group mechanisms, which Bion introduced. I introduced group mechanisms, which were as good as Bion's. One of them was getting rewards for what others advocated and you always opposed. When you voted for Nixon you got a reward for doing things that he always said should not be done, and that others said should be done, and you get a reward for it.

What about the second Bush? Why was he elected twice?

The second Bush is a fool, not an eagle. He was never really elected, because I think the intelligence, the IQ of 300 million people assembled is very low. I don't think that the American public, or the English public, or the German public have an IQ that's a hundred. I think it's way down. Why do you think the German government allowed 6 million people to be murdered while they were looking on? How could it come about? It's unspeakable.

But I don't think it's only a matter of IQ…

No, no, it's about aggression. Aggressive conflict and the murder of the father. Freud explained it, Marx couldn't. I don't think that the social economic classes, divisions, are a better explanation than the Freudian intra-psychic conflict explanations, do you?

No. But you were saying that you were left-wing as well.

Yes, because I think they play a part. I have one of my sons now who's a teacher of art. One of his tragedies is that he doesn't make any money. His father makes money, his sisters and brothers, other people all make money. He sees his sister going on a trip to New York and he gets jealous that he doesn't go and then he says he can't afford to go. He doesn't make enough money. He can't afford to get on a plane, he can't afford a $300 a night hotel in New York. His sister can, I can, he can't. Everywhere he goes, he sleeps at friends' houses. He's a man almost 60 years old who sleeps at his friends' houses. I couldn't do that. So, I don't think Marx is wrong, I think he's not as strong as Freud.

You are saying as well that Marxism has a bit that perhaps is autonomous to Freud.

Oh yes, Marx explains a lot. That's why there's such a rise up against Vietnam, the communists in Vietnam. Capitalist America didn't want Vietnam to succeed so they started the whole war, the same with Iraq. Maybe Iraq wasn't necessary. The second Bush was a fool, I don't think he could think anything through, and his father was no help, his father was no genius. JFK knew what he was doing, and Robert Kennedy would know what he was doing but I think the Bush family were privileged people, they weren't intellectual giants.

But again, they were elected.

Their time came, like Eisenhower, after the war. Eisenhower was popular, you have to get the right white card to be elected. He was there at the right moment, a reaction against the other. When the time matches the man then the two can get together, says Erik Erikson.

What about Obama, the current president? How you feel about him?

I respect him, I think he's smart, I think he's honest and with those two things already you've got a very good president. He's smart and he's honest and he's got a lot of trouble. There's a lot of opposition but he's handing them well. He's making choices that are difficult, but I think that in the end I can't fault him for them. I don't think he did anything dirty to get in. I think he got in, in a wholesome way. He argued his points all along, he was at the right place at the right time. Other black contestants never stood a chance, Jesse Jackson and a few others, but he's this tall, lean, half and half guy, trained in Hawaii at the right schools, he was at the right place at the right moment, that was all.

Do you have any views on the economic mess the whole world is in at this moment? What do you think about the conduct of Wall Street, of the bankers?

There I feel Marx had a lot to say, he will tell us what's the trouble, the unequal division of wealth. I mean one CEO gets his ten-million-dollar bonus. The other persons are unemployed. That's not Freudian, that's Marxian. Has to explain the discontent, that's why you have to respect that too.

Can you tell me a little bit of your ideas about liberty?

Freedom. I made the point here that while politics talks about freedom to vote, the suffrage, freedom of expression, religious freedom, I said the real freedom in the world comes from freedom from internal restraints, like from a harsh super ego or an impulsive id. I said, **"An ego that has mastery provides freedom and gives the individual freedom to choose and that's what analysis is all about. To liberate the ego from determinism by the ruthless perseveration of forces beyond one's control that it brings control into people's lives so that they become masters of their own destiny".** This was an expansion of a phrase written by Waelder himself - Robert Waelder. If you remember, he was the one who opposed my unitary anxiety theory, but he was one of the Renaissance men in psychoanalysis.

In recent years, when the pluralism took hold and my points of view became secondary and not that popular, my papers started to be rejected in the journals. I was rejected by the three major journals: *Journal of the American Psychoanalytic Association* (JAPA), *The Psychoanalytic Quarterly* and the *International Journal of Psychoanalysis*. And several times, each, in a way that I've always found increasingly insulting. The editors wouldn't even answer me. They turned down some, I think, really great papers. One paper was the 'Psychoanalysis of Public Opinion'.

It all started after my position on unitary theory and my position against Arlow and Brenner. Because of that, I lost Henry Smith who was a friend of Brenner, and I lost Arnie Richards who was a friend of Brenner. He has since changed his mind but still it's Brenner. **So, I am still fighting for recognition at the end, for my current stuff, not my old things, not the doll phobia, not the theory of conversion, not the Gilles de la Tourette's disease.** I've written on thousands of subjects but the recent ones, following Nixon, following the Watergate, when I started to write about public affairs, they started to turn them down. Except for Joseph Reppen, who was my savior and published everything I wrote. He took it right away...

Why do you think was that?

I think they were against classical [psychoanalysis] and I became the epitome of the classical. It used to be Arlow and Brenner and I. We were the classical analysts. It ended up only I was, and Blum, a little bit Blum. Not Arnie, not Arlow, not Brenner. I wrote a paper on hypocrisy, I gave a paper here about voting, the intrapsychic dynamics of your vote. When you vote for President of the United States, how much of it is determined by the family you are born into? On what kind of politics your father had? How much of it steeps into you before you even know what kind of politician you are, and where you stand on things? So, they were against all those papers because…

Because they were classical or because they were not clinical?

No, no, not because they were not clinical. I came out openly in the theoretical realm about [how] character traits affect people of importance in our field, like Robert Wallerstein. He is a formidable figure, he's no fool, he's a brilliant, sincere, and nice guy. But his reputation, in his mind, was built on being a democratic scientist not an opinionated, opportunistic scientist. He was a Freudian when Freudian was the most popular, and when Freudianism declined, he became an object relations centrist as a few others. I name Peter Fonagy. He is now the representative of that. Fonagy wrote and I quote this in my book *My Life in Theory*, that, "All analysts who pursue the lifting of repression and the bringing to light repressed memories are fraudulent."

What do you think?

You are surprised at that?

Well, yes.

It's in my book quote page so and so, sentence so and so. He reneged afterwards, he says this isn't quite like Bion, this isn't what he meant. This is what you said, Fonagy. I mean he was against all that because at that time he was the mouth of Sandler, who'd just died. Sandler made him the professor in London that he outlived at the London School of Economics or somewhere.

Now he's known as the voice of empirical research.

Of research, that was Wallerstein, they had that in common.

What do you think about research and empirical research in psychoanalysis?

I think I am as much a researcher, that my laboratory is the clinic, my couch… I picked up a paper called "Activity-Passivity", written by Rapaport, and reprinted by Gill in Rapaport's life collection. That paper was not published until seven years after Rapaport died. And Gill comments that the reason Rapaport didn't publish it during his lifetime is that he wasn't sure of its validity. And he was such a scientist that he wouldn't go into print until he could really prove something. So, he said in that paper, that the capacity of activity-passivity is the most unexplored and the most important determinant aspect of human mentality. It has to do with adaptation, with decision making, with autonomy. Rapaport wrote a lot about autonomy, and independence. Waelder, Rapaport and Fenichel, all wrote about the ego taking control, ego mastery, active rather than passive. In other words, if you are an individual who only reacts to what's done to you, you live your life, and nobody's ever heard of you. If you are a John F. Kennedy, who not only takes in everything that's done but blazes a trail forward and makes revolutionary statements that can't be denied like, "Ask not for what your country can do for you, ask what you can do for your country". You make a statement that is a mystique, it galvanizes the emotions of people. That is a rare active capacity, I think I have it, always thinking ahead, thinking ahead.

Harold Blum has it, Arlow had it, Brenner had it, you have it. You have it by being here. But the passive members of your society or this society are the ones who vote for a Hitler in Germany and let it happen. [They say,] "We didn't know anything". Or the people [guards] in the concentration camp thinking, "I was only doing what they told me to do, I am not responsible, they are responsible", or a criminal who says, "I didn't rape the girl, I just had a sexual disorder. I didn't do anything, it's the brain that did it, or the disorder that did it". This paper explains that the capacity to be active, which you can probably see in some infants, right from the beginning is what sets apart a leader from a follower. The lemmings [are the ones] who follow the leaders into the sea.

We were talking about research…

Oh, yes. So, in that paper Rapaport said there wasn't enough evidence of something, and he said, "what's missing is the thinking process of the research method, the phase of thinking about the meaning of the data". Therefore, I say to you, when I am with a patient or with many patients over many years and I see a pattern, if I don't think about it, I am like everybody else. If I have a capacity to extract the pattern and think about the dynamics, then I am a little Freud. He did that a thousand times. I did it ten times, you do it, everyone does it in the papers he writes. Some more than others and some go off the beaten track and get a little nuts with it. All these people I've mentioned are very important people, but they've all made mistakes. Bob Wallerstein made one big mistake, and I think it cost him his value as a scientist. I told him: "Bob, you've been in this field for now many years why are you saying that no theory is better than anyone else's. Is Carl Rogers as good as Freud? Is Eric Fromm in the same capacity as Erik Erikson? Aren't they different? Isn't one better than the other?" He said, "No, you have to be open-minded". "I am open-minded, one of them is the trunk of the tree, the other one is the twig that falls off" and he stopped talking to me.

But we are back into empirical research. The IPA is currently putting a lot of money into empirical research.

Losing money. What do they get back from it?

That is the point.

Wallerstein stands for research. I don't think he's done any research that I think is so great. By the way, his book on Topeka [*Forty-Two Lives in Treatment: A Study of Psychoanalysis and Psychotherapy*] is criticized a lot because he mixes up psychotherapy and psychoanalysis, and you can't measure them. I am a lifetime researcher in psychoanalysis versus psychotherapy. I once figured how many analytic hours I listened to. I once went into a computer and figured out: 8 hours day, 30 days a month 12 months in a year, how much does it amount to after 40 years. How many hours do you think I listened to free associations on the couch?

Thousands.

There must be about 250 thousand of hours. Does that make me someone with experience? Only if I knew what I was doing in those 250 thousand hours. I know a lot of people who could be there 5 thousand years and I wouldn't pay any attention to what they were saying because they don't have the tools to analyze it, to think about it. Now that's research too.

So, this sort of research is, in fact, a fashion. I am against fashion. I wrote the 'Psychology of Public Opinion', I mean the psychology of fashion. What makes something popular and something unpopular? Why am I unpopular, if I am? You think I am unpopular?

No, you have your own followers.

Why does Fonagy fill the hole or Glen Gabbard?

Well, they are the two most popular perhaps.

I mean analytically, psychiatrically, yes, but analytically should they be?

What do you think about Glen Gabbard?

I think he's a showman, he's a very smooth, college president, fund-raiser kind of type. I mean he's very good for the field in that he's a symbol. He knows how to assemble experts, he edited a book on the principles of psychotherapy, he didn't ask me to be a chapter writer. Could he skip me as a writer about psychotherapy in this day and age? I started the whole field in 1954, 70 years ago, I am still going, but no. Because he's suspicious of the Oedipus complex, he once told me that. He likes me, but he won't get close to me. He's much closer to Arnold Cooper than to me. And what did they do in psychotherapy compared to what I have done? I practically wrote the book on it. I am the original. Leo Stone, Merton Gill and me, we are the original three writers in 1954 on psychotherapy. Not Gabbard, it pains me to see how popular he is and more than him, Fonagy. Because Fongay has made some very damaging statements like "the search for repressed memories is fraudulent". How can he be an analyst and say that?

Klein, Bion, even Winnicott have something in common with Lacan. Can you tell me what do you think unifies them?

They all have the quality of being shocking, provocative, obscure, troubling and challenging. Some of them lend themselves to be caricatured, like I did yesterday when I said that my early exposure to any kind of Kleinian thought processes brought up such ridiculous conclusions that the whole class would laugh. And I would feel that way very strongly. They would give a very complex mental aspect to the brain of the new-born as if it's a highly-developed organ that can work in a complex way. Brenner always pointed out about Kleinianism that some of their claims were incompatible with the stages of development of the brain. That the brain wasn't capable of fantasy formation and integration and future looking and very bizarre and complicated imaginative processes. That the brain was not differentiated enough to justify those conclusions, which was obvious. I think that you need discussion, but more importantly, to me, it was superfluous, in that no data that any analyst ever collected on a couch, to me, supported the Kleinian position. I was amazed at how much of an effect it had in England.

Why did Klein have such an effect in England? Her roots were in Hungary, her training was in Berlin, with Karl Abraham who was a real Freudian as the Kleinians claimed to be, "real Freudians", and then it was suggested to her that she move over to London where there was no such thing as child analysis, there was none anywhere and that she should start it there. Anna Freud was still not there; Anna Freud was in Vienna, a young, young lady at the time, 20 years old. Melanie Klein finds a very fertile soil among these English people who are intellectual but, I am hating using the word, gullible, and in need of a leader, and also in opposition to central European thinking for some reason that I don't understand. That was before my time. Why there should be a competition between intellectual Vienna and sophisticated London? I don't know, but nevertheless that was what grew up historically. Then the Kleinians under Melanie Klein, and stimulated by Melanie Klein, began to report data from dreams and fantasies but mainly, it appears to me in retrospect, fantasies of the analysts more than the fantasies of the patients. That the young infant had the analogue of later thinking by possessing the capacity to have fantasies of destruction and of love combined. It was a primitive kind of love, which was [an] aggressive and destructive love. You have a union of opposites, a union of ambivalent poles, to me it's important to keep the poles and points between the poles. I think that there are many dichotomies that came up in later experience in psychoanalysis in which one was challenged with the same course of action.

To put them… was love and hate to be kept together? Or were they to be kept dissociated from each other? What was normal and what was abnormal? It's normal to have love, it's normal to have hate, it's normal to be able to differentiate those that you hate from those whom you love, it's normal to have a certain kind of overlap between those whom you hate and those whom you love. But to have an indiscriminateness of a kind of mixing of love and hate and life and death… The death instinct became very popular with Kleinians, again poles. They were very interested in opposite polar thinking. I, in contrast to that, saw that a common-sensical approach to what one does with ambivalent opposites is Freud's theory, to me a brilliant theory of complementarity. Both exist, what we see clinically is a tremendous variety of the percentages involved. Is it mostly hate or mostly love? Is it exactly 50/50? Is it a good combination in which each one dilutes the other so neither of them have total sway? I think Heinz Hartmann would lean towards this, towards common sense, towards complementarity, towards the fact that love and hate both exist. Instincts and ego, all these pairings, ego and superego. In any phenomenon it's a question of how much of one and how much or how little of the other. So, what's necessary as one goes along is the choices of which of two poles or to what extent one examines, accepts, either pole as being predominant or operative in a pair. Any individual has to be assessed with how normal are his hate and aggressive impulses. And how normal or abnormal are his sexual and binding, putting together, instincts. How does he live with both being part of his own psychobiological organism? You can't deny either one of them and retain normalcy, if you deny hating anyone or loving anyone you are just whistling in the dark, it's a defense mechanism. Because every analyst knows that every patient is the combination of two, of both.

But I think that in their strong attempts to make one concept dominant in a place and era, they took one *pars* for the whole, *pars pro toto*, they made a part the whole. It moved from Melanie Klein who elected to concentrate on the pre-oedipal, overriding the oedipal, to another phase in America, closer to where I was and more familiar to me than the Kleinian method, the Harry Stack Sullivan theory, which came with the dominance of socialism and communism in the earlier part of the 20th century, and emphasized the inter personal over the intra-psychic.

There was another pairing, intra-psychic and interpersonal, between whole people and the one person broken up into parts, components which were in conflict with each other. Strangely, this same way of thinking of the whole versus the parts, became a third theory with Kohut, who, rather than interpersonal, talked about the self, which was after all the other side of the coin of interpersonal, because interpersonal meant whole selves relating to each other, and the whole, Kohut sensed, was in contrast to an individual segmented, broken up into components, like the structural view which had three major psychic components. But historically, it turned out that every one of those four, Lacan maybe is the best example, was extremely obscure in their writings. Besides being confusing, I would say Klein was not being obscure, she was being confusing. The things she said were bizarre and shocking, but one knew exactly what she said. But it was hard to agree with. On the other hand, you can read Kohut and you don't know what he said when he's all through. Because he said something that is so similar to Freud and yet he thinks it's so different, and this is in character in extreme with Lacan or with Ignacio Matte-Blanco. People just give up on what they read thinking it's too obscure, too un-understandable, to be taken seriously, whereas Freud was crystal clear in his writing. Not only were his ideas revolutionary but they were well-delivered, and one understood them, and one could deal with them. You either disagreed or you agreed but you certainly understood the Oedipus conflict was not obscure. **One wanted something and someone else stood in the way and you got rid of the one that stood in the way and you get to what you want, and that's the Oedipus complex.** Even though people don't like to own up to such primitive motivations. But with Kohut many students end up not quite understanding what they read, but they are Kohutians. A lot of people who read Lacan, they go on about what they read, they never could convey it with logic, but they are Lacanians. Why? Because they are different, every one of them loses, leaves the original territory, sets out on his own, establishes a new land and begins to populate it with new inhabitants. Maybe like the taming of the West in the United States, except here it was certainly all of a different caliber and very welcome and very exciting, very one to be sought, rather than to be shunned. But Lacan I could only stay away from, even though I like Frenchmen. I like the people I knew and some of them were Lacanians and I couldn't understand why they understood him, but later they would change their minds and come around to my way of thinking. That happened with the best, with some of them. I think it happened with Andre Green, I don't think he would admit that, but I think Green acts towards some of his critics, the way he says I acted toward him in 1975. That's some kind of big expanded answer to the simple question you asked about the four different contributors.

Do we analysts, or some analysts, like to be confused? Why do some people prefer obscure theories?

We equate confusion with brilliance, and someone who's clear we think is a simpleton, he's simple but he's simple-ton, he's a fool. Things are too black and white, things are not black and white in nature, they are always grey. So therefore, when we read an encyclopedia and we get dizzy with all the information, we have a feeling we've just read the Bible, even though we can't repeat it. If we read a clear statement in a novel or a short story we may enjoy it, but we don't bow to it with tremendous reverence and awe and respect.

You were talking about your way of doing research, the experience of someone. But why is it that now empirical research, whatever that means, is so popular, really favored by the IPA?

Well, this is the same as the American attitude of 'show me'. The content being something tangible, measurable, it's the whole idea of separating science from non-science and being unwilling to admit that science extends into many obscure areas that are difficult to follow and that are grey rather than black or white.

What about your experience as President of the American Psychoanalytic Association and then of the International Psychoanalytical Association? Did you enjoy the experience?

It was the experience of a lifetime, as much as anyone might complain. Like Heinz Kohut did, who would have liked to be president. Everyone would want to be president. The only ones who don't want to be president are the people who think they can never be a president. Anyone who thinks [he/she] has a chance of being president, wants to be president. I take that as an axiom. Because then the people who deny it - even Arlow denied he wanted to be elected but he never withdrew, and Kohut told me what he did, but it was all a lot of bullshit, you know? Anyway, since I became an analyst I tried to understand the good and the bad in my life through the analytic lens and the same thing applies to political involvements. I learned the practical thing that every single leader needs to compromise, otherwise you can't be a leader. If you're a leader you're a leader of opposite factions, and if you're a leader of opposite factions you have to find viable compromises. When you ask me what I think of Obama, so far, I think he's done well, he's compromised properly. Bush never compromised, you're either for me or against me. That means either you believe in me or you're wrong, I'm right, they're wrong. That's not compromise, that's no leader, that's a dictator. I'm right, you're wrong. Winston Churchill was more of a negotiator. Franklin Roosevelt was a negotiator. I was by instinct a negotiator. I'm the oldest of four children, and each one had love and hate feelings for the one before him. I would say mostly love, I wasn't too aware of hate. My family was a unified family, my folks were old-time immigrants. All they knew was loyalty, there was no question about fidelity as there is today. It was taken for granted, it was part of life, when you got married, you got married, that was your mother and your father. You didn't have two mothers or ten mothers. I have patients that have multiple mothers they don't even know which one they're talking about: my adopted, my surrogate, my step, my ex, my future mother. Which mother?

I had a mother, my mother was from Poland, my father was from Russia. I was from New York as a result of them. They could hardly read English, I didn't have a library at home there, like I have here now. I don't remember a book in my parental home, except maybe the Siddur, my father's religious books were there, that's all. I never saw another book until I went to school. I never in my life had a fairy-tale read to me by a parent, so I didn't know what it was to put your face in a book and have someone recite what was on the words, like today. It's a different stimulus to the brain.

Alright, so I was one of four and I grew up in that environment, in 1913 to 1918-1920. That was a different world than today's world of children and mothers. And I had to live with and adjust to the hierarchy of living, that the oldest goes to school and the next one goes to the same school that the oldest one went to and tries to do the same things that the oldest one does. I didn't know then that the oldest is trying to do the things that the father did. And in my case not so much because we never envied what my father had to go through, he had to go through pogroms in Russia. There was nothing to envy there, he ran away from there to get to this country to live well. I didn't have to try to imagine living his life. I had to try to imagine doing what he would like me to do to make his life worthwhile. He wanted his children to go to school, I went to school, I did well, like he wanted me to. I happened to choose a very special high school in Brooklyn, New York. You wouldn't know anything about this but there was a school in a rather low neighborhood like the Harlem of Brooklyn, the black Harlem of Brooklyn. But in that place was a traditional school that was good in mathematics and Latin. Latin! Of all things, Latin! There was a famous Latin teacher. And I went to that school and I became the AAA Latin student in that school. And I was made editor of the Latin magazine, like you are editor of the IPA Newsletter. I was editor of a magazine called *Forum Latinum*. I was as proud as a peacock. My name was on a masthead of a printed page! I wrote editorials in Latin when I was 15, 16 years old, you know. That was my first education, I was going to be a Latin teacher, that was my aim in life, not a doctor.

Well, gradually I matured. In the midst of anti-Semitism, it was very difficult to get into medical schools. A lot of the people used to go to Europe. Ralph Greenson went to Switzerland to get his medical degree in the same period. But I went to a good high school. I got into a good college, Columbia. That was unheard of at my level of education and immigration. And from there into a good medical school in Chicago, one of the best, and I entered neurology, then neurosurgery, then psychoanalysis. I first knew about analysis, when I vaguely was aware of *The Interpretation of Dreams* in college. I didn't read it, but I was aware of it. And I was aware of the fact that it stressed sexuality. And just like I told you, I immediately took to Fenichel. Later when I was a neurological resident and all the residents started to talk about psychoanalysis, and lot of the teachers were trying to be trained in a place called the New York Psychoanalytic Institute. And I saw that my patients didn't have brain tumors. They didn't all have brain tumors that I could take out and they'd be better. Most of the patients had nothing, you'd examine them neurologically and it was negative, neurological... Were you a neurologist ever?

No.

You'd examine the hysteria, and the conversions and tics and examine and examine and examine. And take X-rays, we didn't have MRIs then, we just had X-rays and negative, negative, negative. I thought when I go to practice "what am I thinking I'm going to do? Extracting brain tumors all day long? I'll be dealing with what we call 'crud'. We used to call old people 'hardware', neurological hardware. Which means they frustrated the poor neurologist who couldn't find anything, they didn't know what to do.

Well, the only people who seemed to know what to do were these people who [they] were talking about [at] the New York Psychoanalytic Institute. They were coming home and telling me stories that were crazy (*laughs*). And again… very innocently, of course, I thought "I'm gonna be a psychoanalyst". Maybe I didn't question it enough, but I slid from one thing into another with very little resistance. The only resistance was that I had to pay this first analyst money. I didn't have any money, and the fee was 7 dollars an hour, that would be like 7 thousand dollars today. I mean, it was out of the question. What I did was I started to "moonlight," do you know what that means? I saw a few patients at night and with all my patients put together maybe I made 4 dollars, and I added 3 and that was my analytic hour. I would take it from the patient and give it to the analyst. I never had anything left over, nothing, zero. My wife was working. I got married early. I was 25, she was 23. She became a secretary and her little meagre existence gave us a little place to live and things to eat. And we were happy as could be. So, I waited and went to the New York Psychoanalytic Institute, there was no question there, that's where they all went and that was the home of Hartmann, Kris and Lowenstein and Phyllis Greenacre and Gregory Zilboorg, and all the big names in classical psychoanalysis. And, of course, I immediately started to learn about them because I was a good student, so I learned about them and for one year I was in analysis. Then I started taking courses and all within a year and a half... Pearl Harbor. The Japanese attacked Pearl Harbor and our country was at war. I was a first-year analytic student, but I was not interested in turning my head away from the war and just being an analytic student, as if there was no war. People were getting killed around me, people were going to the army. Everyone I knew was taking a stance pro and against fascism. It was a time of great revolutionary fervor. And becoming an analyst to me then took its place among other things in life, namely, what I was going to be in New York. Was I going to be a communist or a republican? I knew republicans, I knew democrats, and I knew socialists. Everyone I knew was on the socialist side of things, and further left. I told you that I started to have a conflict between Freud and Marx. I didn't know who was to be my ideal anymore, especially with the war going on. It was more Marx than Freud. Until I realized that Freud would explain the war neurosis, but Marx couldn't.

Anyway, I left New York and went into the United States Airforce, that was the end of my analytic training. I knew I would come back, but I had already in my mind the distant goal, to go to the west coast of the United

States. That's because of an uncle of mine, my mother's youngest brother. who was the only one in the family who didn't settle in New York. He made it to the west. He became a clothing manufacturer and a clothing salesman, opened up a store here on Broadway and he used to come to New York, to buy his suits, by train. There were no airplanes, he came by train. He dressed in a way that was very impressive to me, like he was an actor. And he was just a tailor. But he was a dapper and interesting man and he loved me, he loved me and my brothers. I think he was impotent because he adopted two children. I didn't learn this 'til way later but he was more attached to my mother's children than to his own adopted children, because mine was blood, the other ones were not blood. So, he loved all of us but me the most because I was the oldest and I identified with him, not with my father but with him. And I wanted to go out West where he was. Now the war takes me in an airplane away from New York, the Airforce. In my mind was "I'm never going to come back here, I'm gonna go there [to Los Angeles] after the war", which I did four years later. I was part of an exodus, just like the exodus to Israel, they were all going to southern California.

Without needing to cross the Red Sea.

No, I crossed the American continent. You can't imagine the stories I could tell you about what the West Coast meant to me at that time, and the fantasies that developed. Towards the end of the residency we were once in a cloak room and one of the young neurologists was very anti-analytic. He was one of those who stood against this whole wave of people who were going to the NY Psychoanalytic Institute, a brilliant guy named Nathan Savitsky, who talked, talked, and talked about the beauty of the brain and he was a specialist in multiple sclerosis. And he picked me, and I was a bright resident, so he picked me and told me: "Hey Rangell, come here. Do you want to write a paper? I'll put your name on a paper, "The Ocular Findings in Multiple Sclerosis" by Savitsky and Rangell". I didn't know nothing about that, they were his cases, but I helped him write it a little bit and he put my name on it. The journal comes out, Savitsky and Rangell, I mean, I was in heaven. I didn't even know what the hell I was writing about, but it was like a taste of seeing your name in print. It meant a lot to me then.

So then after, we were in a cloak room and Savitsky was carrying on about psychoanalysis and there was a man in that room who was finishing his residency, and I was coming in, it was his last day and my first day. We were in the residents' cloak room, where you put your coats, in the winter, and this guy had everyone sitting around him and he said "Hey, hey Engelberg, you're going down West out there. Do you know what kind of place that is? You ever hear of George Gershwin? He died of a brain tumor, they told him he had hysteria because they were psychoanalysts. That's what goes on, on the West Coast", Engelberg said. He was Hyman Engelberg, the guy who would give Marilyn Monroe the chloral hydrate by which she committed suicide. The story was that Gershwin was in analysis and that his analyst was telling him he had hysteria and it turned out he had a brain tumor. This was supposed to be against analysis and for neurology, if you understand and follow me. This was before the war.

Many years later, when I came to LA for the first time in uniform, through Tuli, my wife's uncle, I was invited to a party at Ira Gershwin's. And they say "Hey, who are you?", I said "I was a neurologist and was training to be a psychoanalyst when war came, then I went into the army and now I'm here". "Oh", he says, "You can't be a psychoanalyst. You must know about my brother, George", And I said, "Tell me about him." He said, "Oh his analyst was a guy named Gregory Zilboorg". And Zilboorg was a neurologist who kept telling his patient, "you've got organic symptoms here, you should see a neurologist" and the neurologist was sending him back as hysteria, and the analyst was sending him back [to the neurologist] as a brain tumor. This I heard from Ira Gershwin, it was the complete opposite of what Savitsky had told me in New York.

That's a very interesting story.

It certainly is a fascinating story. Recently someone showed me the case history of George Gershwin at the hospital where this was confirmed, that Eugene Ziskind said he had hysteria and that Zilboorg said he had a brain tumor. And I was always, always, very alert to not missing one for the other. And I thought it was very good to be a neurologist and a psychoanalyst because you never miss a brain tumor if you're an analyst who's a neurologist first. By the way, I never became friendly with the Gershwins. I was too shy to capitalize on that contact. I moved away from them. They never heard from me again, you know? Other people became friendly with them, not me.

How do you see psychoanalysis developing in the future? You mentioned first the medical part and then the non-medical people coming in, now what?

I see that people will be more fair-minded as time goes on and recognize the validity of the Freudian revolution in 1900. I think what Freud discovered then, and what was first accepted and then minimized between 1900 and 2000 is going to be rediscovered. I think that fair-mindedness and the need for survival of the human race will bring back all those things that were rejected and [we will] learn that some of it is to be accepted and mastered by the part of the mind responsible for mastery, and that's the part that Freud was talking about, and none of these can be measured. We are going to have to come to terms with the fact that beyond the brain there is a lifetime of thought processes, which are not recorded in the brain or the heart or the bones, and that when the organism dies every thought process that that individual had is gone away into thin air. Einstein's thoughts were completely gone the moment his heart stopped and he stopped breathing. Freud's ideas are completely out of reach. We can't get any more ideas out of Freud after 1939 because his brain stopped. But the derivatives of the brain, every frame of life, is a result of that man's being alive, and which some people can only explain by saying there's a God, and to other people that's no explanation. We don't know the explanation, but there's no God, it evolved; this universe evolved. Man has an evolutionary history. Plants have an evolutionary history. There's no man with his beard in the sky, who waved his right hand and there was Adam and then waved his left hand and there was Eve. Thinking man does not at the moment believe that, but Freud pointed to something, which, as much as it told us, it also presented puzzles. I am spending my life trying to understand the border between the brain and the mind, that's the area of the psychoanalyst and it's far from being described as yet, but it's a concept that we have, that I have. And it's the subtitle of one of my recent books, the book on music *Living at the brain-mind border* [Full title - *Music in the Head: Living at the Brain-Mind Border*]. It's how the music, the involuntary music started in my head [After open heart surgery, in his mid 70s, Leo Rangell began hearing music coming from outside his head. It was a symptom of a mild anoxia he suffered during the surgery. He heard music coming from outside his head for the rest of his life.] I am looking to see how the brain changes sound to music. No one ever figured out that yet. The brain registers auditory stimuli loud, soft, persistent, staccato, shrill, pleasant, unpleasant. What makes all those things come together into a symphony? What makes a Beethoven take all those sounds, or a Tchaikovsky, and make rhythms and tunes that you can't get out of your head anymore - once one of them gets in there? One of my books was about that, about how I am the subject of that. That music book is a very, very provocative creative little book but it's on the same subject, living on the brain-mind border, and my interest is beyond the brain. I told this to Oliver Sacks, and he respects it and agrees with it. He can't answer the questions any more than you or I can. He can answer the logical questions but not the psychological ones. So, we are in a very challenging and very provocative and very gratifying field in thinking about those things. In the future they will come closer and closer to solutions than we are now.

Do you think that solutions will appear?

We will come closer to solutions than we are now. I don't know what the solutions will ever be. I don't know that you will ever see a fantasy on a slide.

The Kleinians might think...

And the neuroscientist might think, Mark Solms might think, but I don't think he will. I don't think you will ever see a mathematical formula written in the cortex.

And what do you think is the difference between Oliver Sacks and Mark Solms? One is a neurologist, the other a neuroscientist...

I am very biased because I am a neurologist too, and I had a period when I was intensely interested in the anatomy of the brain, like Freud was interested in the anatomy of the medulla. But I was interested in that, as well as the rest of the brain, because I thought that all the solutions to life can be demonstrated in the brain. Well, it didn't take me long to realize, even as a young neurologist or neuropathologist, that no matter how much you study the human brain, you will never, never see brilliance in a brain or stupidity in a brain. Although with autism you see some changes at that end of the spectrum, but you never can tell. People say, if you had the brains of Einstein and Hitler side by side you couldn't tell the difference. My interest in this is as a former neurologist, present psychoanalyst.

And Mark Solms and Oliver Sacks are brilliant examples of pushing neurology further and further towards understanding this dilemma. Freud tried in his "Project" and failed, these people are trying to do it.

Will they fail?

Freud failed, they are trying to do it. They didn't give up, they don't think they will fail, no. They are still doing it. However, I don't think within our lifetime there's going to be any significant breakthrough in the border between the brain and the mind. I don't see anything leading to any thought that we will ever see a change in chemistry relating to a change in thinking, in fantasy, a discovery of something or of the absence of something. You will never find "Oh, here's Einstein's formula", "Here's Beethoven's symphony", "Here is the guy who invented polio vaccine".

I think that this is a great way to end our conversation, and I hope that we can take it up again at some point in the future. As always, it has been a pleasure and a privilege to listen to you. Thank you very much.

It has also been my pleasure. You're invited whenever you'd like; you know that you're always welcome.

International Psychoanalytical Congress, Vienna, 1971;
J. Van de Leeuw, Jeanne Lampl-de Groot, Anna Freud, & Leo Rangell

Otto Kernberg

Rudolph Lowenstein

Harold and Elsa Blum

Martin Bergmann

Leo Rangell and Beth Kalish

Leo with Saúl Peña and Marcelo Viñar, then President-Elect of the Federation of Psychoanalytic Societies of Latin America, at the 41st IPA Congress (Santiago, 1999)

Leo with Saúl Peña, editor and translator of the Spanish edition of The Mind of Watergate, and Claudio Eizirik, then President of the IPA, at the book presentation (Santiago, 1999)

Leo with Francisco Morales Bermúdez, former President of Perú; Saúl Peña, Honorary President of the Peruvian Psychoanalytic Society; Beatriz Boza, then President of the Peruvian Commission for Promotion of Export and Tourism; and Otto Kernberg, then President of the IPA, at a lunch reception of the International Conference At the Threshold of the Millennium (Lima, April 1998)

Arnold Richards

How did you become an analyst? What happened in your life that put you on this particular path?

Believe it or not, my earliest lexical memory I can date to age five. It was reading or being read *The Forward*, the Yiddish newspaper. There was a picture of Sigmund Freud and the headline was "Famous Jewish Psychiatrist Dies" so it was September 1939. Actually, a few years ago I looked up a copy of the paper from that date and there was the picture of Freud and the headline. The bearded man may have reminded me of an older orthodox man who was the landlord of our building (by the way, I have had the same kind of beard for many years). Was this transference? I was a precocious kid. I read a lot. I could read Yiddish and English at an early age. I am not sure whether this was a screen memory or a retrospective falsification. In elementary school I read Aldous Huxley, *Point Counter Point,* Pearl S. Buck's novel about China, *The Good Earth,* and Flanders Dunbar's text on psychosomatic medicine, *Emotions and Bodily Changes.*

I know the book well because Flanders Dunbar was the analyst of my first psychiatric teacher, Carlos Alberto Seguín, who trained at Columbia.

I was interested in reading the book because I had hay fever, a severe case. I got the message from that book that understanding of the unconscious and conflicts could help me cure it. When I was sixteen I read Freud's

Introductory Lectures and it was then when I decided I would become a psychoanalyst. I also read the A.A. Brill translation of *The Interpretation of Dreams*. Both books, it turned out, determined my future. Growing up, I went to public school and Yiddish after-school. I connected with a bearded, orthodox Rabbi, and believe it or not, I can hardly believe it myself, not only did I get Bar Mitzvahed, I also became orthodox: praying two times a day, putting on *tefillin*.

Why?

That is a good question; I am not sure I know the answer. Perhaps it was a way to deal with pubertal pressures. At the same time, I was engaged in orthodox Jewish ritualistic obsessive practices, in high school, in Brooklyn, Erasmus Hall (four of my classmates there became analysts, Bennett Simon, Stanley Palombo, Martin Willick, and my wife, Arlene Kramer Richards). I was reading Henry Miller, James Joyce, Kenneth Patchen and many other *avant-garde* writers. I applied to many colleges including Harvard and I was accepted at all of them, but I could not afford to go to any of them. I started at Brooklyn College, which was free. It was there when one day a letter came in the mail from the University of Chicago offering me a full scholarship. Of course, I accepted, I met my wife there, and the rest is history.

You were a New Yorker originally?

When I started at the University of Chicago it was the end of the Robert Maynard Hutchins Era. I arrived in October of 1951. Hutchins had left the previous spring. The first person I met on campus was Ernie Hartmann, the son of Heinz Hartmann. I remember him because he seemed to look to the side and mumble. Many years later when I saw Heinz Hartmann at meetings of the New York Psychoanalytic Society, he also looked to the side and mumbled.

Perhaps some people who read this might not know about the University of Chicago program.

The University of Chicago College had a program based on the great books. All the readings were from original sources. The emphasis was on the philosophy of knowledge. Richard McKeon and Mortimer Adler were the originators and gurus. The final course in the curriculum was called Organizational Methods and Principals of Knowledge (OMP). The idea was to learn how to think rather than to acquire particular specific knowledge, which you might use in a profession. The program has been watered down since I was there, but the University of Chicago is still an exciting place. We had the motto, "The University of Chicago: where fun goes to die". And it is of interest that the university's ranking has increased from ninth to fifth this year. They have a system where you take exams for all the courses, and only have to take those that you don't place in. I placed in everything, but I had to take four courses; I got my degree in a year. In retrospect, I think that was unfortunate, because I missed a lot.

But getting back to my religious orthodoxy, Arlene told me that she had heard about the student who would wrap leather around his arm. Maybe it was a turn-on for her. Anyway, we met, we went out to our first date in January 1952, we went to a Polynesian restaurant, I ate shrimp for the first time in my life, and my orthodoxy was over. But I still had becoming a psychoanalyst in mind.

Or a rabbi?

Or a rabbi. Actually, at the University of Chicago I considered going into mathematics instead of medicine, and in Medical School I became interested in internal medicine and neuroanatomy. The wish to become a psychoanalyst moved to the background. I also got interested in forensic psychiatry. By the way, our son is a criminal lawyer. But there remained the wish to become a psychoanalyst. I was part of a cohort of individuals like myself, Jewish intellectuals, who perhaps today would go into finance, but then went into medicine and psychoanalysis. Psychoanalysis was a way to combine an interest in science, and an interest in humanities as Freud did.

But you say someone like you today would go into finance?

Right! They are less likely to become physicians or academics. Most of the children of our group did not become psychoanalysts. The fifties were the halcyon days of psychoanalysis. For many of us it was the ticket to ride. It was an interesting, intellectually stimulating activity and I think many of us read Freud in high school. In one of the exams, they used a paper on Freud and we had to answer questions about his thinking and his theory. Freud was a part of the culture in the fifties and sixties. The psychoanalyst was often portrayed in the movies. Psychoanalysis then was very different from what it was when someone like Charlie Brenner was going into psychoanalysis in the nineteen-thirties. At that time, only mavericks pursued that esoteric occupation.

I had a summer clerkship between my second and third year in medical school at the Marine Hospital in Staten Island. Larry Deutsch, who was a candidate at the Downstate Institute, now New York University (NYU), and in analysis with Melitta Sperling, was my mentor. Sperling was interested in psychosomatic medicine. She was so convinced that she would cure psychosomatic illness with psychoanalytic interpretations that she would visit a patient in the hospital and remove the IV from the patient's arm saying "You know what you are doing? You are ingesting your mother and turning her into shit". This interpretation was supposed to cure the patient of their ulcerative colitis. Larry Deutsch had this incredible belief and enthusiasm in the power of psychoanalysis and some of his enthusiasm influenced me.

After Medical School, I interned in Baltimore, Maryland, at a public health service hospital. Our next-door neighbors were the Polands, Warren and Janice. He, at that time, was a psychiatric first-year resident at the University of Maryland. Jake Feinsinger was the chair. He [Warren Poland] had the same enthusiasm about psychoanalysis, which he conveyed to me in a very personal way. On the first day of my internship and his first of day as a resident, he told his wife who was pregnant (I hope he doesn't mind me saying this) "Whatever you do, you know when I am in session I can't be interrupted."

He had his priorities right!

When I got home his wife was about to give birth. I was called to assist. I had an OB clerkship in medical school and sort of knew what to do, but the birth was spontaneous. I only had to catch the baby and I tied the umbilical cord with a string from her skirt. The Polands remain our closest friends.

The positive psychoanalytic ambiance at the University of Maryland was important. At that time many of the chairs of departments of psychiatry were psychoanalysts. If you wanted to get ahead in psychiatry you needed to have analytic training. After my internship, my interest in psychoanalysis did not waver. But first, I had to become a psychiatrist.

I applied to the Albert Einstein College of Medicine and I think I was most interested in it because several of my friends went there. It had a very psychoanalytically oriented program. Milton Rosenbaum was the chair. Herbert Weiner and José Barchelon were on the faculty. Many of the residents were in analysis with training analysts from the New York Psychoanalytic Society and Institute (NYPSI). I was interviewed and accepted but decided that with a wife and two children I couldn't afford to go, given the salary, which was provided. I didn't really want us to live in a basement in the Bronx during my residency. I didn't think that that would be a great life for my family. I decided to go to the Menninger School of Psychiatry in Topeka instead. I liked their brochure. I didn't go there for an interview. I still remember the sinking feeling that I had as I drove down from Kansas Avenue. I said to myself, "What am I doing here?"

What the fuck am I doing here?

Yes, what the fuck am I doing here in the middle of nowhere? What's a nice Jewish boy from Brooklyn doing in Kansas? Well, there we were and the next thing I know I get a call from Harvey Bezahler. He's an analyst and again one of my good friends. He was a third-year resident at the time. He trained at Downstate and is now one of my best friends. His job was to orient the new residents. I quickly came to feel at home and comfortable in Topeka. I think I did make the right choice. In retrospect, I think it was better for me than the "*echt*" psychoanalytic cookie-cutter model of Albert Einstein. Even though I did my training at the NYPSI, I was able to preserve a certain degree of independence in thinking because of my Menninger training. The fifties and sixties were also halcyon times in Topeka. Many of the greats had left: David Rapaport, Roy Schafer, Robert Knight, Merton Gill. But others were still there when I arrived: Howie Shevrin, Herb Schlesinger, Sybille Escalona, the Wallersteins, the Tichos, the Murphys. Some psychologists became training analysts because of Karl Menninger's clout in the American Psychoanalytic Association (APsaA). Menninger Clinic was a terrific analytically oriented residency, but it was also a wonderful place for another reason. I mean also culturally, believe it or not.

In Topeka, Kansas?

Yes, culture in Kansas. They had a program of visiting professorships sponsored by Alfred P. Sloan from General Motors. He gave money to get visiting intellectuals to spend a month in Topeka. Konrad Lorenz, Ludwig von Bertelanffy, S.I. Hayakawa, Margaret Mead, Max Gittleson, Chuck Fisher, Peter Kuper, etc. gave lectures to the residents. I have the list somewhere. It was a remarkable experience. Instead of the rather narrow rigid training at Einstein, I had a training, which was eclectic and open to the wider world of ideas.

Karl Menninger wrote *The Human Mind* in the thirties, and it became the bestselling psychoanalytic book for the lay public ever written. He was a very interesting person. I'll tell you about how Menninger got started. C. F.

Menninger, the father, wanted to emulate the Mayo brothers. He wanted his two sons, Karl and Will, to become physicians and work in his clinic. They went to Harvard. They got interested in psychiatry and when they came back to Topeka they started the psychiatric clinic, the Menninger Clinic. Their father ended up doing physicals on their psychiatric patients. Will probably did more for the development of American psychoanalysis than anyone else. He was in charge of recruitment for the Army during World War II. He made all these mostly Jewish doctors, psychiatrists. They treated the war wounded and shell-shocked with hypnosis. When they left the Army in 1946-1947 many of them decided to become psychoanalysts and many decided to get analytic training in Topeka. There must have been 150 applicants for their training program in one year in Topeka. Will and Karl really didn't get along, siblings often don't. Will spent most of his time on the road raising money and Karl spent his time running the Menninger Clinic

We had Saturday morning sessions in which Karl interviewed patients; he was writing his book at the time *The Vital Balance*. We read it chapter by chapter.

Karl had his own take on psychiatry, he didn't believe in nosology. He believed in the vital balance, he believed in understanding people as individuals and not as diagnostic labels. He was also very much interested in the larger world. And that helped me specifically, because he established a program with James Bennett for the Federal Bureau of Prisons, and as a resident I was on active duty in the public health service. You were paid as an officer and then you had to work in a prison for two years. This was a pretty good deal for me because it was two years rather than four years as in the Berry plan.

Karl, as you know, was the first graduate of the Chicago Institute. His analyst was Franz Alexander. He took the train from Topeka to Chicago and had four sessions in two days each week to become a psychoanalyst. Will also trained in Chicago. In some ways Karl Menninger, a Presbyterian who grew up in Pennsylvania, was more Freudian than Freud. He was one of the few American psychoanalysts who believed in the death instinct. His book

Love against Hate had to do with Eros and Thanatos. He communicated to us his enthusiasm for psychoanalysis and for understanding people. He and Alexander, his analyst, went off to see Freud and the story goes that Alexander left him in the waiting room. Alexander told Freud that he shouldn't pay much attention to Menninger. Of course, Menninger was very hurt by this. I don't know exactly what was going on between the two of them and there were some complicated aspects. I think it was Karen Horney who analyzed his [Menninger's] wife who left him. That's the usual kind of stuff that went on in those times.

And today?

But I'll tell you what I meant about culture. Since there was no culture in Topeka, we had to bring it to Kansas. I became the chair of the Menninger School of Psychiatry Film Society (I followed Leon Levin and Otto Kernberg followed me). We showed *Hiroshima Mon Amour* and screened *The Threepenny Opera* before it played anywhere in the United States. We rented the best foreign films. There was also a Chamber Music Society run by Philip Holtzman and Herbert Schlesinger.

How long did you stay in Topeka?

Three years. Karl wanted all the residents to return but somehow, he let me go. He would get angry if you didn't return and work in the Menninger Foundation. I am not sure why that wasn't an issue in my case. Perhaps it was because I went to Petersburg, Virginia where I became the Chief Medical Officer and Chief Psychiatrist of the Federal Reformatory, so I was in charge of the medical treatment of all the inmates and of the staff. My main treatment modality was group therapy to help the staff understand psychological forces at work in their daily encounters. I also did pre-sentencing evaluations for the court. I was in Petersburg from 1962 to 1964. Those were very exciting times in the South. The civil rights movement was in full swing and Petersburg was very much on the front line. In fact, they closed the schools to avoid integration and set up whites only private schools. We sent our kids to the Bollingbrook Day School and I was elected president of the parents' association. Not sure why, I think it had something to do with the fact that I was Jewish and a psychiatrist. I was encouraged to stay in Petersburg after I finished my tour of duty and start a private practice. They were aware that segregation had discouraged professionals from settling there.

How did that connect with psychoanalysis?

That's a good question because to me one of the problems with psychoanalysis is its disconnection with academic communities and the cultural surroundings. I think you are an exception.

The connection between psychoanalysis and social issues was natural for me because I was interested in politics, since I was a teenager. I think it was also the case of Otto Fenichel and people like him in the United States.

The members of the Freudian left you know: Otto Fenichel, Henry Lowenfeld, Edith Jacobson, Barbara Schneider-Lantos, Francis Deri, George Gerö, Lilo Gerö-Heyman and Annie Reich. They had been politically involved in Vienna. Russell Jacoby said, "When they came to the United Stated they dropped their politics in the Atlantic Ocean." They became democrats. They loved Franklin Delano Roosevelt, even his dog Fala was an icon. As they became successful and made money they moved away from social consciousness and socialism. Edith Jacobson and Wilhelm Reich were communists. Jacobson belonged to the German anti-Hitler group the New Beginning. She was arrested by the Gestapo for refusing to give information about her leftist patients. Lilo Gerö-Heyman was able to get her out of jail by telling the authorities that she had to be in the hospital because of diabetes. She was able to escape to Prague after that.

Were they afraid? Wilhelm Reich did go to prison in the United States because of his orgone accumulator. He was a bit crazy, as well… I wonder if it was not fear that made them move away from their beliefs.

They were afraid in the forties and the fifties. This is the time of McCarthy. They were very grateful to the United States. They knew they were lucky to be alive. As analysts they carried the mantel of Freud and this gave them a certain cache at analytic institutes in the United States. In New York it was the Europeans who really took over from the Americans. They were in a very good position in the institutes, which meant lots of patients and lots of money. They rapidly rose to the top of the psychoanalytic economic ladder.

So, they dropped their ideals in the Atlantic?

The story of the role of the Emergency Committee on Relief and Immigration of the American Psychoanalytic Association, chaired by Lawrence Kubie and Bettina Warburg, in facilitating the immigration of European analysts before WWII started, is worth retelling. All but two, Kurt Landauer, who died of starvation in a concentration camp, although his daughter survived, and one other. All the members of the Viennese Psychoanalytic Society were rescued but not all of the candidates. Do you know why? Because there was no roster of candidates, so graduation was a matter of life and death.

On the other hand, American psychoanalysts of the same era, like Jack Arlow, Charlie Brenner, Eleanor Gallenson, Milton Jacoby, or Larry Roos made money in a capitalist system but that did not preclude them from leftist convictions. There was a communist cell at NYU in the early forties, the list of psychoanalysts who belonged or who were sympathetic is long. They had grown up in the depression and had a strong aversion to inequality and championed social justice. They raised money for the Lincoln Brigade and two analysts, Aaron Hilcovich and William Pike went to Spain. The Europeans, with the exception of Wilhelm Reich and Edith Jacobson, had an aversion to communism based on their firsthand experience. Do you know Shelley Orgel?

No.

He was the Chairman of the Board of Professional Standards (BoPS). His father was Dean of Students at Lincoln High School where he was a student. He joined the Communist party in college. He was part of a cohort of American Jews who became psychoanalysts after joining the party in the thirties and forties. I think Jack Arlow was the last to leave, having maintained his allegiance through the purge trials and the Ribbentrop-Molotov pact. He was William Z. Foster's personal physician. Jack would not leave the country because he was concerned they would not let him return. My wife was in analysis with him. She once visited my father in the hospital and the next session spoke about how she could not understand that anyone should be so stupid as to remain a communist after the thirties! Jack left the Communist party after the Duclos letter, which had to do with the refusal of Earl Browder to knuckle under to communism. "Browder is our leader and we shall not be moved" was the song then.

Some leftist psychoanalysts replaced communism with Zionism as an ideology. I think some of them brought to psychoanalysis the same sense of certainty that was manifested in their politics.

They needed a complementary ideology, to be an analyst was not enough.

For some of us, yes. That was true. It was certainly true in Red Vienna where psychoanalysts were socially conscious. They set up clinics for low cost treatments and every analyst was expected to participate and donate some time. The sense of social consciousness there was strong. Elizabeth

Danto wrote about this time in her book *Freud's Free Clinics*. The Viennese (and Berlin and Budapest analysts) entered training with their left political commitments. My generation in the US was less politically active. They spent 8 to 10 hours every day in their offices seeing patients and making money (also teaching and supervising) and did not have much time for social activism although they did see low fee analysands as part of their training. Senior analysts were not expected to see low-fee, non-candidate, private patients as in Vienna, Berlin and Budapest, but there were some individual exceptions, Kurt Eissler was one. He also expected others to do the same. He would refer me patients for low or no fee and I usually accommodated them. Several years ago, one of those patients left me $1000 in her will, which I received after she died.

On the other hand, a group of psychoanalysts organized by Charlie Brenner and Buddy Myer —more than 100— took out a full-page ad in the New York Times during the Vietnam war protesting the Gulf of Tonkin Resolution. I think many psychoanalysts marched and protested. When we were in Petersburg, Virginia, Arlene went to the Civil Rights March on Washington. She got up at 4 a.m. and went to the Ebenezer Baptist church where she joined Wyatt T. Walker minister. She and the Jewish Chaplin from the Fort Lee Army Base were the only two white people on the bus. I was very frightened on that trip. I think my generation was very activist and socially conscious during the Vietnam war. The communist-socialist divide had passed.

Was any analyst that you knew in the Lincoln brigade?

No, but besides Aaron Hilcovich from Chicago and William Pike from New York whom I already mentioned, twenty-five percent of the members of the Lincoln Brigade were Jewish, most of them from New York and more from Brooklyn than the Bronx, Queens or Manhattan, I don't know why.

Those were the children and grandchildren of the first Jewish immigration, lots of them were socialists.

That's right. You know my parents are from Europe as were Jack Arlow's parents, and Charlie Brenner's as well. They certainly didn't talk about their left political commitments.

Why? Did they abandon them? Were they afraid?

Psychoanalysts were not supposed to talk about their personal life or their politics, because that would impact on the transference. I don't know how much that generation knew about each other's politics.

At the NYPSI there were two groups, the ins and the outs. The ins ran the place. The ins were mostly Europeans like Otto Isakower, Ruth Eisler, Kurt Eissler, Lillian Malcove, Nick Stein, Robby Bak... I'll tell you a joke. When Bak was Chairman of the Education Committee he said, "I never took a majority vote lying down". When Otto Isakower was the chair, there were seven women on the committee, Phyllis Greenacre, Ruth Eisler, Annie Reich, Bettina Warburg, Lillian Malcove, Ruth Loveland and Mary O'Neil Hawkins. Someone asked: "Dr. Isakower, what is like to be Chairman of the Education Committee with seven women?", Otto —who was very short— replied: "It's like seven Snow Whites and one dwarf." Otto was a very interesting man, he published 29 pages and became a phenomenon. He went from Berlin to Liverpool, England, before he came to the United States. I always wondered whether his Liverpool connection was why he loved The Beatles.

The politics of the NYPSI was divided between the Europeans and their supporters. Martin Stein and Phyllis Greenacre were not European, but they came out of the tripartite Berlin model, the training analysis was central. The structures were authoritarian, fundamentally anti-democratic and self-perpetuating. On the other side were Jack Arlow, Victor Rosen, Charles Brenner, David Beres, Martin Wangh... the Americans who were not part of the in group. People are amazed when I tell them that Jack Arlow was never on the Education Committee nor was Charlie Brenner. Since they couldn't make it at NYPSI they invested their political energy in the American Psychoanalytic. Jack Arlow was never President of the American, but he did serve as chair of BoPS. There was also a consequence for the politics of the International Psychoanalytical Association (IPA) in 1969. Do you remember who became President of the IPA in 1969?

Leo Rangell?

Yes. And do you know who wanted to become president? There wasn't an election in those days.

No, no, it was a sort of consensus.

And do you know who decided? Anna Freud decided who would be the president. Heinz Kohut very much wanted to become President and he thought it was a done deal. He had selected his Secretary, Francis Hannett, Gittleson's wife.

Kohut was from Vienna. He told everyone that he went to the train station when Freud was leaving Vienna and that Freud tipped his hat to him. Freud went to London and Kohut went to Chicago.

I think August Aichhorn was his analyst in Vienna and Ruth Eissler in Chicago.

He developed his own ideas...

Yes, but this was in 1969, before he wrote *The Analysis of the Self*, which was published in 1972. Leo Rangell insisted that Kohut became a self-psychologist because he experienced not becoming President of the IPA as a narcissistic blow. But the fact is that Kohut developed those ideas before 1969. I know the real story. I was able to read the correspondence between Marianne Kris, Ruth Eissler, and Miss Freud about the Kohut matter. Kohut's dream was to become President of the IPA and he was ready to have that dream fulfilled when he was told by Anna Freud "You have to withdraw in favor of Leo Rangell because the Europeans don't want you and we are afraid that Arlow will run against you and be elected." In one letter, Rangell was referred to as the "lesser of two evils"; the greater evil was Arlow-Brenner.

By the way, Jack assured me he had no intention of running for president of the IPA. As I mentioned before, he was afraid to leave the United States because he was afraid he would not be allowed to return because of his Communist Party connection but I don't think that was an issue in 1969. Jack told me he remembered having a meeting with Martin Wangh, David Beres and Charlie Brenner about whether he should run and they all advised him not to run, apparently Ruth Eissler was not aware of that. Her fear was that Jack would run and win and that the IPA would give the Arlow-Brenner group more political clout and that would affect the balance of power at the NYPSI.

So local politics were more important than the rest of the world.

Of course, that is if there was a 'rest of the world'. Did you know Phyllis Greenacre was against APsaA publishing a roster because people would think that everyone on the roster were real psychoanalysts? For her, the only real psychoanalysts were the psychoanalysts at the NYPSI. This reminds me of the story about Winnicott. He was giving a paper and he put a revolver on the lectern. He said: "That's for the person that says I am not a psychoanalyst."

Because his last paper was the one on the use of the object.

Yeah. It's a long story. He came from London, landed at the airport in the rain and no one came to pick him up. He got pneumonia and had to be hospitalized. Milton Malev, a member of NYPSI paid his hospital bill. He died soon after that. What killed him, the criticism or the pneumonia?

But to return to the 1969 IPA election, Anna Freud didn't like Arlow also because he was for Board Certification for psychoanalysis and not sympathetic to lay analysis or child analysis. Why was Anna Freud so influenced by Ruth Eissler and by Marianne Kris? Miss Freud needed money for the Anna Freud Center. Marilyn Monroe was in analysis with Marianne Kris and was encouraged by her other analyst, Ralph Greenson, to give money to the center. Doug Kirsner has written about these relationships. Not psychoanalysis's finest hour. Royalties from Monroe's estate were a major source of the Anna Freud Centre's income.

You're referring to a period in which the power that psychoanalysts had in the psychiatry departments in the United States began to peter out. Were they so involved in fighting each other they didn't see what was going on?

That's a very good question. To what extent was it our own doing and to what extent did it have to do with factors beyond our control: pharmacology and managed care? The fifties and the sixties were the halcyon days of psychoanalysis. It was what I called the "psychoanalysis a plenty", plenty of patients, plenty of candidates, plenty of prestige and plenty of money for psychoanalysts. Leo Rangell practiced in Los Angeles and treated Hollywood stars who could afford high fees. But, in Los Angeles there was an effort to destroy the Kleinians. It was led by Ralph Greenson and Milton Wexler and Leo to some extent. The internecine warfare diminished our ability to present a united front to the world at large. In the fifties and sixties, we promised more than we could deliver. People expected to be magically altered by psychoanalysis and were disappointed.

When it was believed that an interpretation could actually cure colitis.

That was one issue, the other was arrogance. Dick Simons, who was President of APsaA during the lawsuit, wrote in the Journal of the American Psychoanalytic Association (JAPA) that APsaA was not guilty of antitrust violations, it was guilty of arrogance. The arrogance was institutionalized with the reorganization of APsaA in 1948, and the establishment of the BoPS, a self-perpetuating body who would decide who was a good analyst. This was not an attitude that is consistent with the development of a science and a profession.

Those were who came after the socialists. I mean, those arrogant people who actually perpetuated themselves in power positions.

They were not the socialists. Who were they? Was it the Berlin Eitingon model, which had its firm stamp on psychoanalysis? They functioned more like the Communist party in terms of democratic centralism.

I think it was the model.

The Certification Committee is the membership committee of BoPS. They decide who is eligible to become a training analyst. Only training analysts can become fellows of BoPS and elect the BoPS chairs who in turn appoint the Certification Committee that determines who can become a fellow and elect the chairs and so on and so on. It wasn't always that way. Before 1948 there was a Committee of Psychoanalytic Education whose decisions had to be supported unanimously by the institutes. It changed because Sander Rado had left NYPSI and established a new institute at Columbia. There was a concern that Rado would have a three-times a week training standard. There was also a concern that William Allison White would want to join APsaA with people who were not physicians. If you review the minutes of the BoPS and the APsaA —for decades— the mantra is the same: it is not "What can we do to advance psychoanalysis?" It is "What can we do to keep people out? What can we do to make rules? What can we do to set standards? How rigid can we be? My major effort as a psychoanalyst and a psychoanalytical political activist has been to try to change that system.

In the beginning political ideology participated in the development of psychoanalysis and then suddenly it did not.

It drops out.

And then it was as if you're an analyst you should be only an analyst and withdraw from hospitals, from universities and other public and private venues. Psychoanalysis constructed an ivory tower for itself. We are paying a heavy price for that even now. I don't know if you agree with that.

Yes. I'll give you some specific examples. When Charlie Brenner wrote a letter to the New York Times about the Vietnam war he was attacked by the members of NYPSI because they said his action would disturb transference. Analysts shouldn't be doing that. There were analysts who were also working in hospitals that couldn't become training analysts because they weren't committed enough to the private practice of psychoanalysis. One of my classmates was Herbert Pardes; he probably is now one of the most important psychiatrists in New York if not in the United States. In fact, the Psychiatric Institute at Columbia University has been named after him. When he graduated, he couldn't become a member of APsaA because he did not want to apply for certification. That didn't make any sense to him. He resigned from NYPSI and APsaA and went on to become one the most important psychiatrists in the United States.

In a sense, people who run the APsaA, and I think it is the same in different parts of the world, became psychoanalytic fascists. I am not sure if it is the right word... There was a change of ideology.

It all began in 1948 with the establishment of BoPS, which became more exclusive as time went on. When I applied for certification I sent in my cases and got a letter back saying I was certified, this was in 1972. As time went on the procedure became more onerous and they added interviews. Some say it is more like a fraternity hazing than a collegial process: 50% fail the first time but 95% pass with persistence. So, what is the point? Is the test a valid and reliable test of psychoanalytic competence? What? A ritual with no objective criteria for making assessments?

It was just to keep people out. Then little by little, drugs appeared in the sixties and so forth. Were they fighting the wrong enemy?

That's right. I don't know how we can understand the psychology of the people who move the organization and maintain the organization in that kind of hierarchical authoritarian direction.

After the Institute for Psychoanalytic Training and Research (IPTAR) joined the IPA and IPTAR members could become members of the IPA and APsaA, my wife, Arlene Kramer Richards, became a member of APsaA. That pleased me a lot because it had always been my ambition that Arlene could become a member of every organization that I belonged to. I almost made it with the exception of the NYPSI because they have a requirement that you can't become a member even if you are member of the IPA unless you've been trained at the APsaA Institute. Andre Green couldn't become a member of the NYPSI, nor Moisés Lemlij even if you moved to New York. I fought for decades to get them to agree to train social workers. They finally agreed last year.

But getting back to Arlene, after she became a member of the APsaA I told her "Why don't you get certified? We are actively encouraging members of IPTAR and the Freudian Society to join the APsaA and we wanted to show that all their procedures were fair." She flew to Toronto to be interviewed by the Certification Committee. The member of the committee to whom she presented her cases, made no eye-contact. At the end of the meeting he said "Now, I have what I need." She thought that meant that she had been accepted. No, she was rejected. Keep in mind that at that time Arlene was a training analyst at two institutes and several of her analysands became training analysts themselves. But the committee decided that she was not a competent analyst.

I felt badly that I had put her through this. I was editor of JAPA at that time, so I started a discussion about the certification procedure. I began the discussion with a quote from Bob Michels paper, "A Psychoanalytic Case Study", in which he said that the purposes of the Certification Committee and the purposes of the Committee on Scientific Activities are mutually incompatible. He was saying that certification is not scientific. At the time of that discussion if you weren't certified you could be a member, but you couldn't vote, and you couldn't hold office and you couldn't be a training analyst. So, it was a very active discussion back and forth and finally a bylaw amendment was passed. The first delinkage allowed uncertified graduates to become members; the second delinkage allowed all members to vote for everything and run for office. This was a very important change. More recently we submitted a bylaw (Institute Choice) that would allow institutes to appoint members who were not certified. But I remember Sandy Abend, who was from New York and someone I've known quite a long time, said to me "Arnie, I will never forgive you for what you did". "What did I do?", I asked. "You provided a voice, a platform for the people who should not be talking about education."

What exactly did he mean?

He meant that the members list was a platform where ordinary folk, the uncertified, those who were not training analysts, the unwashed and the unanointed, those not part of the educational establishment, could talk about the pros and cons of certification. For some, APsaA is divided into alumni and faculty. The members are from the alumni association and the training analysts are faculty. Another friend, Leon Hoffman, said he will also never forgive me because I destroyed psychoanalytic education.

That was democratic centralism, which is of course the least democratic of all systems because it perpetuates the Stalinian elite until it dies.

The Coordinating Committee of BoPS is composed by the chairs of BoPS and the chairs of the BoPS Committees. The committee chairs are appointed by the chairs of BoPS and the Coordinating Committee meet four times every year. This small group decides BoPS policies, which are then approved by the full Board that meets twice a year. They think they are protecting psychoanalysis from the barbarians — me, Judy Schachter, Paul Mosher, and others. We are the bad guys who are intent on destroying psychoanalysis. By the way, someone who was elected BoPS chair was thrown out of APsaA for boundary violations, Ralph Engle. And one of the recent BoPS chairs said that an uncertified member would become a training analyst over her dead body.

Do they believe that if psychoanalysis is not kept "pure" it will be destroyed?

I really think that mostly it has to do with power and being in charge. They just want to stay in charge. I think it has more to do with power than with principles. I don't know to what extent this is a conviction and to what extent this is a rationalization. They are convinced if they are not in charge that it would be bad for psychoanalysis. When change is imminent, they threaten to leave the organization. They're gonna take their marbles and run. But they don't have a place to go and they won't leave.

They want to keep things as they were in 1948 in 2010.

It's 60 years, it's amazing.

What amazes me is that most analysts have tolerated this situation for decades.

Well, part of it is that if you knock your head against the wall long enough enthusiasm is replaced with apathy and you leave. Nothing can change, so why bother? They are very well organized. They have a machine. They talk to each other. They tell people how to vote, who to vote for or who to vote against. It is like the Daley machine in Chicago. I know first-hand because I was once part of the in-group at NYPSI. They have telephone trees. Their incentive is that their livelihood is based on the training analyst system. Their patients are candidates. And once in power, people are reluctant to stand up against them because the fear is that you won't get faculty appointments or referrals. Real or imagined, actual or magical, fear keeps the system in place. I was able to become an activist in APsaA when I became editor of JAPA. Some said I was improperly using my position to give credibility to the opposition who were posting on the members list, but I saw it as my position enabling me to act against the "compact majority". I thought I was doing it for principle. In the end, Marx was right.

Money.

Yes. Don't underestimate how money drives people.

It looks as if it was, for you, a crucial moment when you became editor of JAPA.

I think you are absolutely right. How did I become editor of JAPA? First of all, I owe a lot to Homer Curtis. Homer Curtis made me the Editor of the [APsaA] Newsletter. It had no name when I took over. Helen Fisher came up with the name: *The American Psychoanalyst*. Most people felt I did a wonderful job for three years.

How come? I mean, how did he choose you?

Why did he choose me? At that time, I was part of the establishment. I think Shelley Orgel recommended me. I was not known for being political. I trained at NYPSI and was involved in Downstate/NYU, as well. I didn't have a track record as a writer or editor. I was a new achiever. Also, around that time Ed Weinshel was supposed to write a paper for the *Psychoanalytic Quarterly* on the future of psychoanalysis.

He was the treasurer of the IPA.

Yes. Ed Weinshel was a very good friend of Shelley Orgel and he got sick and I wrote the paper "The Future of Psychoanalysis" for the *Quarterly* instead of Ed. It was well received. Charlie Brenner liked it, Jack Arlow liked it. I was a good writer and I had good ideas. I had the right friends in high places.

As I said, I did a good job as editor of *The American Psychoanalyst*. The first issue was dedicated to the 50th Anniversary of the death of Sigmund Freud. I did a lot of historical stuff during the three years I was editor. It became a very engaging newsletter. Lots of interviews and other substantive stuff I didn't want it to be just a house organ. So, then the question of becoming editor of JAPA…

Who was the editor then?

The editor was Ted Shapiro.

Why did you apply?

Why did I apply? I was encouraged by Jack Arlow and Charlie Brenner. I always had an interest in writing and publishing. I applied for the position. Ed Weinshel was the Chair of the Search Committee, but he got sick and Jack Arlow took his place. Now some people maintain that I got the job because Jack Arlow was Arlene's analyst. The committee included Otto Kernberg, Arnold Goldberg, Herb Schlessinger, Phyllis Tyson and Harry Trosman. In the running were Bob Michels, Ethel Person, Warren Poland, and Bennett Simon. Poland and Bennett Simon sort of dropped out. Ethel Person wanted it very much. Fortunately, Otto, who favored Ethel couldn't make it to the meeting in which I was interviewed. Otto and I had a big falling out because of the IPA election. I supported Hanly who was running against Otto —which is another story. We knew Otto and Paulina when they first came to Topeka. Paulina was a resident with me at Topeka, so I would probably have known Otto longer than anyone else in the APsaA. Arnold Goldberg voted for me even though I had written some very critical papers about self-psychology. In any case, I made a terrific presentation to the Search Committee. I told them things about the journal that they didn't know themselves. Everyone there was positive, and they voted for me. I was told it was unanimous in the end. I was appointed editor in 1993.

That gave me standing in the sense that I was not beholden to anybody. Through self-publishing I increased the revenues of the APsaA by about $900,000. Not chump change as they say. Circulation increased as well as revenues. When I took it over we increased circulation to 4000 from International University Press (IUP), the publisher. At our high point we reached 5,200. When I became editor a lot of the increase of subscribers was from outside of APsaA, from people I knew, from IPTAR and the Freudian

Society and William Allison White. My approach was to break down walls and become more inclusive. I gave a paper about the politics of exclusion (The Brill Lecture at NYPSI). My thesis was that the shadow of the founder falls over an organization. APsaA's founder was A.A. Brill who was adamantly against lay analysis. APsaA was exclusive in regard to other matters as well. I was determined to be inclusive.

Becoming editor gave you political power because you could publish and give a voice to whoever you thought fit.

I felt secure enough in my psychoanalytic professional position that I could afford to take controversial stands that wouldn't be approved by everybody.

You increased revenues and subscriptions but then things went back again. This must say something about you and something about the organization. They were not able to maintain what you created or maybe your time was the exception and the real self of The American Psychoanalyst was the one before and the one after you.

I have a reputation for being open and inclusive. The original plan for the PEP CD-ROM was to include five journals: JAPA, The Psychoanalytic Quarterly, The Psychoanalytic Study of the Child, The International Psychoanalytic Journal, and the International Review of Psychoanalysis. Owen Renik and I said we need to include Contemporary Psychoanalysis, which is the journal of the William Allison White Society. David Tuckett, the editor of the International Psychoanalytic Journal said that he never heard of Contemporary Psychoanalysis, or the William Allison White Society. We said that from the point of scholarship and subscribers more journals would be better. (Now most psychoanalytic journals are included).

I wrote, in my introduction to the first Symposium of the PEP CD-ROMS, that the search engines would bring us together. The symposiums were very successful because they were eclectic and inclusive. We had

Kleinians, Relationalists, Self-Psychologists, Freudians, Jungians, and others. Our symposia were much more successful than the programs for mental health professionals run by APsaA. My view was there was a larger world out there and we had to invite presenters from other groups and from other orientations. Freudian contributors outside APsaA were reluctant to submit their papers to JAPA because they thought they would not be accepted. My first year as editor I published five papers by members of IPTAR. The rate of acceptance of the papers by IPTAR was higher than for any other group. I think circulation increased because of the expanded authorship.

When did you begin to relate to the wider psychoanalytical world?

That's a very good question. If I look at my own background, I had to go back to my father who was a Bolshevik. He was a librarian for a unit of Trotsky's army.

My father was a Bolshevik, as well.

In Trotsky's army?

No, no.

My father deserted the Red Army in 1920. He got typhus and was hospitalized in Odessa. He met some Jewish doctors who encouraged him to go to medical school in the Soviet Union. He would be one of the new Soviet men. He went back to his hometown to tell his father of his plans. His father told him he needed to leave Russia because the Bolsheviks were just as anti-Semitic as the Czarists. My grandfather was a very wise man. He told my father that he hoped someday he would be able to help his two sisters to leave, as well. He deserted the Army and crossed into Rumania in the middle of the night in a small boat with his gun on his lap. In Rumania he joined a Zionist youth group and went to Palestine. He was in Nahalal (Moshe Dayan's *moshav*), worked draining the swamps, got malaria and left in 1924 for the United States. I don't really consider myself a red diaper baby because my father was not politically active, but I was sympathetic to the left as most Jews of my generation were. I was always concerned with social justice. I don't do well with exclusion. I'm big on my civil rights activism, in Petersberg, Virginia, as I have already told you about. I've always felt connected to the larger world. I didn't want to just have an office, treat patients and be oblivious of what's going on in the society around me.

What about the morals, the moral stand for American psychoanalysts, the idea that if you were working in a hospital you could not be a training analyst?

Exactly, right! Their justification was you wouldn't have enough time to see enough patients. It took Ed Shapiro a long time to become a training analyst because he was working in a hospital.

How did this sort of international background of yours translate into psychoanalysis?

I guess you know I'm very involved with Yiddish. I was Chairman of the Board and Director of YIVO Institute for Jewish Research. Many say that the only reason I got involved in the certification discussion was because of my wife's experience. To some extent, that's true, but I don't know if I would have the drive and the commitment without my own imperatives. I have the sense that the American Psychoanalytic Association was given a precious gift by Freud and that we have squandered that legacy because of our arrogance, lack of humility, authoritarian structures, and the politics of exclusion. Whether that accounts for the fact that there are institutes who don't have any candidates and candidates who don't have any patients is not clear. Was it the rigidity of the theory in the hands of some or the fact that the training was not patient centered? The patient has to come four times a week to meet the institute requirement. The patient had to fit the Procrustean bed. Irwin Hoffman told his patient she had to lie on the couch because he wanted to graduate. There is a whole system of conformity and compliance. In the end the patient loses out.

And all of this because of the shadow of Brill...

Psychoanalysis was mostly a medical discipline in the United States because of Abraham [Arden] Brill, who was a poor boy from a *shehtl* in Poland. He came to the United States at age 13 with two dollars in his pocket. Becoming a physician and a psychiatrist was his way of making it in the New World. And he did. Medicine was his ticket to ride. He established the medical identification of psychoanalysis in the United States. The NYPSI and APsaA excluded non-physicians, some of whom might have been more fertilizing. A problem now is that psychiatrists for the most part are not interested in psychoanalysis and the ones who are interested are rather dull. They don't have a humanistic approach. To be a good psychoanalyst you have to be a *gebildet Mensch*. Freud's *Bildung*, his interest in archaeology, history, literature, and the wide span of human culture contributed to making him the psychoanalyst he became. Also, his Judaism. Not ritual and observance, but the ethical system and its roots in the Enlightenment, in the *Haskalah*. Brill had none of that. You can make a case that Brill and APsaA adopted the medical model out of insecurity. Was the board certification model of medicine adopted by APsaA for that reason? It is an interesting question. Did they feel they had to have standards because they were insecure about what they were doing? Freud was insecure in a different way. He felt his theory was at risk from dissidents and heretics like Jung, Adler, Stekel, and others.

Do you believe that this was what allowed psychoanalysis to hold such an important place in society in the United States?

Well, right now psychoanalysis is more part of the culture in Argentina.

Of the culture, but not of the power structure.

And in France it's also part of the culture more than in the United States.

But it isn't part of the French establishment.

Which establishments are you talking about?

Universities and public health institutions.

There is no question that it became part of that establishment in the United States until the sixties.

And then arrogance and hubris…

They could afford to do this exclusion because they were pretty much sitting pretty again. There was a psychoanalysis of plenty and they were very secure, and they wanted power and they wanted to maintain their power. Theodor Reik was at the NYPSI but they wouldn't let him become a full member, so he left and started the National Psychological Association for Psychoanalysis (NPAP). After a while he was referring patients to members of the NYPSI.

Now let's go back to your story. You finished Topeka?

Right, I finished Topeka and as I said it was a very important part of my psychiatric and psychoanalytic development, and to my relationship to non-medical analysis. It was a very good clinical residency. Then I went to Petersburg, Virginia, where I was the Psychiatrist and Chief Medical Officer at the Federal Reformatory. A psychiatrist in a prison is not the model of a psychiatrist in a private office. My effort was to have an impact on the prison environment. I worked more with the staff than with the inmates. I did decide to apply for analytic training either in Washington or in New York. I applied to the Washington Psychoanalytic Institute, and to the Columbia and New York Psychoanalytic institutes. I did not apply to Downstate in Brooklyn because I went to medical school at Downstate. My teachers in psychiatry were from the Downstate Institute: Shelly Orgel, Sam Abrams, Leonard Shengold, Austin Silber… They were *gung-ho* about psychoanalysis.

The fire?

The fire, yes. Some of it came from them. So, I didn't apply to the Downstate institute because I was from Brooklyn. I guess I didn't want to go home again. I wanted to live in Manhattan. I didn't want to commute.

My interview at the Washington Institute was an interesting experience. The committee was Dan Jaffe, Edith Weigert, and Harold Searles. Harold Searles said: "I see you are working in a prison. Is that because your childhood was a prison?" Edith Weigert came to my defense. I had three interviews at New York. My first was with Bernard Fine. Each interviewer saw the applicant three times. The second was Andrew Peto, he was Hungarian. A lovely man. I told him I had a dream the previous night. In the dream someone said to me "That's fine".

Lili Bussell was last. At the end of the third interview she said: "Dr. Richards, now I understand your case." That, of course, meant that I had passed. She had determined that I was analyzable and therefore was acceptable for the training. The year I applied there were 40 applicants and they accepted 13. My class was 12 men and 1 woman; 12 psychiatrists, 1 psychologist. The psychologist was from the NYU Center for Research in Mental Health. He had to sign a statement that he wasn't going to practice.

We had terrific instructors like Rudolph Lowenstein, Otto Isakower, Bert Lewin, Edith Jacobson, Margaret Mahler, Nick Young, Chuck Fisher and Charles Brenner. Those four years were great. I did very well —you know I'm good at doing well in school. I also started my analysis. My analyst was Henry Lowenfeld. He was part of the Freudian left. He was in the Weimar Government in the twenties. He was very smart. He left Berlin in the early thirties anticipating Hitler. He went to Czechoslovakia. He had the foresight to leave early. I had the occasion to talk to his son because someone from Europe wanted to do his father's biography. His son asked me: "Oh, when were you in analysis with my father? Did you help pay for my college education?" He told me a story about when he was 2 years old leaving Berlin. His father found a sign for the car which said *"Judden sind unger unglück"* (Jews are our misfortune). He thought that was why they were able to proceed without being stopped. My analyst was quite *Kosher*. I wonder if there was some way he conveyed to me his own involvement in the left.

Was he German?

Yes, German. He was very different from the usual American analyst in terms of his political background.

He knew what it was like.

And I'm sure something got conveyed to me. Analysts responses can encourage some views and discourage others. I began my training in 1964 and graduated in 1969. Five years, not too bad.

...but exceptional!

Very exceptional. My first supervisor was David Beres. My first case was a person who had hypochondriacal delusions. Analysis went well. My second supervisor was Theodore Lipin. He moved to Sweden and died there. He was analyzed by Lillian Malcove. She said: "even I didn't understand him". Many found his writings totally incomprehensible. Of the 12 people he supervised only two survived: myself and my friend Lester Schwartz.

Why did you choose him?

He was assigned. At NYPSI you don't choose your supervisors.

That's so un-analytical. In most countries you choose your supervisor.

In fact, I didn't choose Henry Lowenfeld. I was assigned to Ruth Loveland. Do you remember her?

And what happened?

She said we would start and then she said that she couldn't because a patient who she thought was terminating didn't. Perhaps it was alphabetical — Loveland, Lowenfeld. My third supervisor, George Gerö, was a wonderful European, different from Lipin and Beres. Lipin attended to the minute by minute process, Gerö was more on to the big picture: the organizing unconscious fantasy and so forth.

After I graduated, I attended the affiliated staff conferences. The usual thing was for the Europeans to say that the patient was severely disturbed and un-analyzable. The Americans, like Charlie Brenner and Jack Arlow, thought differently. Every patient had conflicts, which you could try to understand, whether it would help or not. That was 1965-1966. I then continued my post-analytic education at the Madison Delicatessen on 86th Street and 3rd Avenue where we had lunch once a week, Charlie Brenner, Bernie Brodsky, Sandy Abend, Mervin Peskin, Arlene and me. We would discuss psychoanalysis. Now I remember it must have been around 1972 that Charlie said to me, "You know this fellow Heinz Kohut? He has written a new book. Read it and let me know what you think".

You mentioned Otto Kernberg in your days at Topeka. He has developed very influential ideas. I don't know if one can call them a school but certainly he must be one of the most familiar names of American psychoanalysis today.

Yes, Kohut and Kernberg had two different approaches to narcissism and narcissistic disorders...

That was in the seventies, but your disagreement with Otto was not theoretical but political.

With Otto my political disagreement was not until the Hanly Election. What year was Otto elected president? [Otto Kernberg was President of the IPA 1997-2001]

Around 1993 or 1994.

Yes, because it was after I became editor of JAPA. I had a very good relationship with Otto until that time. Paulina called up Arlene and said: "Are you voting for Otto?" and Arlene told her she was going to vote for Charles Hanly because he did a lot to help IPTAR. Otto and Paulina got very upset with us because we supported Hanly.

Did you support Hanly because of Arlene?

Yes.

That's a different chapter.

I was on Otto's side because, in my view, unlike Kohut I felt conflict was more important than deficit. I titled the *Festschrift*, I edited for Charlie, *Psychoanalysis: The Science of Mental Conflict.*

You are not that convinced about that…

I believe that conflict and deficit are interactive variables. Conflict leads to deficit and deficit impacts on the way conflict is experienced. I have a problem with dichotomies. That was my problem with Stephen Mitchell and Jay Greenberg, their drive vs relational dichotomy. I think the reason Freud has survived as well as he has is because he never came down on one or the other side of a dichotomy. It was always nature and nurture, conflict and deficit. He had a complex view of human mental functioning.

Otto had referred me patients. We were close to the Kernbergs socially and we sold them our first house in Maine. But I guess it was Arlene's falling out that became the problem between us.

I participated a lot at the IPA when he was president. He made important modifications. He eliminated the House of Representatives that Horacio Etchegoyen established and organized the current Board of Representatives, which is elected regionally. While it appears to be democratic, I don't think it is. I think the House of Delegates allowed a better representation for societies and their memberships. But that's a different story.

I tend to agree with you because I do sense right now a distance between the IPA and most members of the APsaA.

But the APsaA has never been too close to the IPA. Something that comes to my mind is that because of the regional rotation the current president is a Canadian, not an American, and the previous president from North America was Otto who is really marginal to the Americans in many ways. He was not an American mainstream representative. So, I think for the last 20-30 years there have been no real representatives of the American. I think there might be something important about this because maybe half of Latin American psychoanalysts vote in the elections but only 10%-15% of American psychoanalysts vote.

And mostly from the non-IPAs institutes in the USA, correct? There is a long history. Look what happened in the thirties with the International Training Committee. NYPSI said they were not going to let the IPA tell them how to train and who to train and took a very strong stand against lay analysis, which was enshrined in the Maresfield Garden agreement. APsaA was not going to subordinate themselves to any organization including the IPA. APsaA and BoPS would be a law unto themselves. There was very serious consideration of having a Board of Psychoanalysis. Jack Arlow and Charlie Brenner were in favor, but it got sunk because of the fear that if they had become part of the American Psychiatric Association as a medical specialty board, they would become subservient to them. No one was going to tell them who to train, and how to train. Everyone outside their circle was excluded, a small number of people ran the show. Those not in power become apathetic or dropped out so the majority of the ruling class increased. The opposition got marginalized or melted away. Psychoanalysis paid a heavy price for this.

Where is the APsaA right now?

I think the APsaA has a problem. They are talking about having one national meeting rather than two, membership is declining, members are getting older, the dues base is going down, the number of candidates is decreasing. They're fighting over a system to allow psychoanalysts who haven't been trained in the APsaA to become members. They are trying to define functional equivalence, but BoPS is the naysayer in this effort. If we won't take people from the outside and we have fewer new members from the inside (our own graduates) our prospects are not very good.

So, the big enemy of American psychoanalysis is the BoPS.

The big enemy in the APsaA in my opinion is the small number of people who control the BoPS. I have a friend who died last year who said to me "You know, Arnie, we've had a good ride. Who cares about what happens next?". They would rather maintain the purity and the power of their position than do things that would benefit the organization as a whole. I am not sure I understand what motivates those people. But one thing is sure, I am certainly *persona non grata* among those folks. I have been called a loose cannon and a gadfly. One member of the NYPSI said: "Arnie we need you to be a gadfly, but we don't want you to drink hemlock". I see myself differently. I feel I'm trying to save them from themselves. I like the quote from *The Leopard*: "If you want things to stay the same, they have to change". I did convince the NYPSI to train Masters of Social Work.

It took 15 years during which I was considered a loose cannon clinically, maybe politically... I mean, I tried very hard and finally I've succeeded in getting them to train them, but it's been about 20 years. BoPS adopted a new certification procedure, which was an improvement but not enough. There's no transparency.

What is the current make-up of the APsaA membership?

Probably the largest consumers of psychoanalytic treatment and training and practitioners are social workers. That's the trend in the United States in my opinion. So even among psychologists it's becoming less the thing. There is an upside, from what I've seen among some of the candidates. Since psychoanalysis is not a very lucrative profession with a lot of prestige, we are beginning to now see people going into training who are committed to the endeavor as they're not motivated by these other things that motivated people in the past. There are some people that are really attracted by the intellectual challenge of psychoanalysis: to understand how the mind works.

This may be because of one's own experience in analysis, and there are some analytic enterprises that are very exciting. *Philoctetes* sponsors meetings and round tables with psychoanalysts, academics, poets, neuroscientists. My point is that the profession is not as attractive as it has been in the past but there remains an inherent excitement in plumbing the depths of the human psyche. I wrote in my paper on "The Future of Psychoanalysis" that psychoanalysis will provide concepts for the neuroscientist to discover rather than neuroscientists just finding ways to validate our concepts.

I think that's great. Have you been in touch with neuroscientists?

I just read them. And I have a lot of stuff on my website www.internationalpsychoanalsyis.net which talks about these connections. Unfortunately, I don't go to the neuroscience meeting because it's on Saturday, we're up in the country on Saturday.

Can you explain to me a little bit more about the fact that we, as analysts, think or conceptualize something and then neuroscientist might find it interesting?

For example, the psychoanalytic concept of defense. We should have some neurophysiological correlates. Charles Fisher was a pioneer psychoanalytic neuroscientist. He had some ideas about dreams and REM sleep. He went into the laboratory and discovered the penile erectile cycle. There are some studies that have demonstrated a connection between loss and panic disorder, which should have neurophysiological correlates. Our clinical experience is that early loss has a profound impact on development. Donald Klein, among others, has been looking into the neurophysiology and neuropharmacology of loss. Trauma has important developmental sequelae. My point is that psychoanalytic concepts derived from clinical experience can provide fodder for neuroscientific studies.

You were saying, in a way, that we analysts may make interesting contributions to neurological sciences, but this does not necessarily mean that we are going to profit from what they discover. So, in a sense it is the other way around. Because some people may think that neurophysiological discoveries may be beneficial for us analysts, but you are saying that it is the other way around.

At the moment I'm taking that position. That's my point. But we may benefit from the interaction with people in other sciences. For decades we kept aloof from other disciplines and we paid a price. It impacted on our prestige and we got fewer patients that way because when we connect with academics and show them we understand something, they may end up becoming our patients, as well.

What do you see in APsaA's future?

There are things that concern me a lot. For example, the NYU institute has disconnected from the NYU Department of Psychiatry. The Department is interested mostly in money and grants. I am not sure how long the Columbia Institute will stay connected to the Columbia Department of Psychiatry after Herb Pardes leaves. NYPI has a loose connection with Mt. Sinai but it is essentially free standing. At Columbia the main source of candidates are psychiatric residents. They go into training for a low-cost analysis and many drop out before they finish classes.

But it is as if you feel more hopeful about the non-APsaA societies.

Yes, IPTAR is doing quite well because they have a program of re-specialization. They take people who are not physicians or psychologists, give them clinical experience under supervision, and make them into psychoanalysts. Some are from overseas and come with student visas. I hear that they are a lively group: smart, interested, and committed. In the 1930s, things were different in the United States. Psychoanalysis didn't have status in the culture. Those who went into analysis for treatment or training were interested and committed and now... It's very hard to predict the future. I like to quote the young girl that Selma Fraiberg treated who said, "Dr. Fraiberg, you are very good in backwards fortune-telling".

Prophets of the past.

So, the question you raised is how can we develop a more vibrant profession when there's more that's interesting, attractive, and exciting to people who have ability, intellectual interests, and clinical skills?

Obviously, you are interested in publications. You increased the readership but somehow you were not able to teach your successor how to do that part of the job.

Let me talk about what I did that was successful in JAPA. First of all, I redesigned the cover: new logo, new graphics. I feel very pleased that my successor has kept my design. We had a different color for each season so if you looked on your shelf you could identify the recurrent issues —Summer, Fall, Winter, Spring. I was also trying to make a statement that JAPA was changing. My aim as editor was to give the journal a voice. I wanted to forge a relationship between myself as editor and the readership. I liked to do thematic issues: papers from different authors talked to each other. I ran JAPA as a collective. I like collectives. My associate editors were Glenn Gabbard, Phyllis Tyson, Larry Friedman, Harry Smith, Bonnie Litowitz. All were actively involved. Every paper was read and responded to within three months, four months max. That's not what is happening now, I am told. I rarely, if ever, overruled the judgments of my three readers. Some journal editors do just that. I would always try to mediate the differences of opinions. Some papers would go through three or four revisions before they would be accepted. I had a file of dozens of letters sent to me by rejected authors telling me how much they appreciated the critique. I also liked doing supplements, theme issues, and anniversary issues. I published plenary addresses with commentaries. I developed an internal interactive format to engage the readers. I was trying to forge a connection with the readers. If readers feel that the journal has an identity, they are more likely to maintain their subscription. A journal should be more than a series of papers. The current editor has several other jobs including Director of the Institute, and the Head of the Department of Psychiatry.

You mean an editor has to be an editor and that's it.

Correct. Other editors told me they spent five hours a week on the job. For me it was a 24/7 job. I was involved in every detail including production and marketing.

How much were you paid?

$25,000. Do you know that story? They had removed the stipend and I was ready to start with no stipend. There was a meeting with the Executive Council and Ted Shapiro came and said: "This is ridiculous, you have to pay the editor." and then someone from the Executive Council said "This is ridiculous! JAPA will be on your bookshelves long after you're gone." The Council voted to restore the stipend even though I would have worked for no money.

What happens now?

JAPA is now much more medically oriented. More research papers are published although I'm very underwhelmed by some of them.

I think part of the reason why a lot of people voted for Charles Hanly is because he is a non-research person. However, he raised the budget *for research, so in a way he has disappointed a lot of people and now there is a lot of money each year given to two things: the school of Peter Fonagy, where people are trained for research, and to people who actually do research. More than half of all the money in the IPA goes there while for instance cultural endeavors only get $20,000 a year.*

I always thought that is what happened when Otto Kernberg was running against Charles. Otto promised Bob [Wallerstein] he would give him money for research if he supported him. I think for the first year Bob did get $150,000 for research. Is that correct?

It might be. I don't know the amount, but I know that in a way, he was in charge of that budget. There was a committee to assess projects but basically, he was the chair.

Is there any effort to evaluate the cost-effectiveness of these projects in terms of psychoanalysis?

When I was the Treasurer, I did write exactly that. I suppose that was one of the reasons why Otto was so strong against me on several occasions. Peter has been asked to justify and he did edit a publication, which has 300 copies, with a review of some of the research but basically there has never been a review of the research projects that have been subsidized with millions of dollars.

It's my feeling that we should spend money on cultural programs to connect with real people and give them some sense of what psychoanalysis is about. Some may seek training or become patients. I'm always interested in doing things that bring organizations into the community and connect them with people. That's what psychoanalysis needs right now. Otherwise, it will become a dinosaur, a relic.

I don't understand why Charles has continued that policy.

I had the sense that somehow, he was taken by David Tuckett and Peter Fonagy. How did that happen?

I don't know.

When Charles wanted me to be on his committee for the website, he let me know that he wanted Tuckett, as well. I think he views him as an expert. But I never did get on the committee.

Anyway… I wonder how you would describe your own psychoanalytic ideas.

In terms of theory, my approach is patient centered. You follow the patient rather the patient following you. Theodor Reik wrote about listening with the third ear, I would add listening with the fourth ear. Listening, being mindful of everything you know about different theoretical approaches to the patients' pathology. The fourth ear includes not only different psychoanalytic psychological ideas but also neurophysiological concepts. And it is not enough to be right, you also have to be helpful. You always try to understand what has caused the patients' difficulty. The patient who gains understanding is different. The patient has changed. Brenner is more specific about what constitutes change. Charlie has a much more specific idea about what you are trying to do, namely, help the patient have more pleasure, less anxiety, less guilt and better adaptation. Another broad framework.

You know how to achieve that.

You ask yourself "Have I achieved that"? You have an idea about what you are looking for. But there is not only one way. In every instance with every patient you need to determine why the patient is unable to have pleasure, why he/she has too much anxiety, has too much guilt and not enough adaptation.

If you try to understand that with your patients perhaps even the process of trying produces an improvement.

That's my conviction and you need to have conviction to do this work. Einstein said that if you don't have a sense that it is possible to figure out how the universe works, why bother? You can't have a totally relativistic approach to your patients. You have to have a sense that you know something and that what you know can be conveyed to the patient and will be helpful. But also figuring out why a certain understanding doesn't lead to change can also be helpful. I think I have changed along with my patients. I see patients now in a much less rigid, open fashion. Why do they say the patients now are less neurotic?

They say you find more depressive and more borderline patients now. That they are different from the classic neurotic ones.

All I can tell you is that when I was in training the patients were just as borderline then as they are now and just as depressed then as they are now. As for the widening scope, the patients haven't changed. Who we are willing to treat has changed. I've seen patients who supposedly were psychotic, *meshuggah,* until you get to know them as individuals. Patients are hungry. They need a connection with someone who is dedicated to trying to understand them and help them rather than use them or misuse them.

You use meshuggah as a broad clinical definition. That brings me to your connection with the Jewish mind, to Yiddish as different from Jewish in general. I mean, you were talking about your Bolshevik ancestors, about the centrality of being a Jew.

The fact is psychoanalysis is a quintessential Galitzianer enterprise. The first fourteen analysts in Freud's group were from Galicia themselves or their parents were from Galicia. Now how do you account for that? And Freud's whole life and work was played out, in my opinion, in the context of his *shtetl* origins and has a relation to anti-Semitism. That's where psychoanalysis began.

The relation with anti-Semitism. Explain what you have in mind.

Anti-Semitism was very much part of Freud's life and experiences from 1880 on. Freud joined the B'nai B'rith where he presented some of his work. He wanted to be part of the Gentile establishment, part of academia, but that was impossible because of anti-Semitism. When I was a candidate we had classes on Yom Kippur. I was one of those who insisted that we shouldn't have classes on Yom Kippur. They were all trying to be assimilated rather than recognize their own identity. How does that impact on an analysis? Kohut denied that he was Jewish. After he died, one of his analysands told me he felt betrayed because Kohut would not acknowledge that he was Jewish and when he died his analysands and his colleagues found out.

He was supposed to have left Vienna…

So? But he got Bar Mitzvah and wouldn't tell his colleagues that he was Jewish. He would make a point of going into a Kosher restaurant and ordering a ham sandwich as if he didn't know. He was a deceiver. He would not acknowledge that he was the analysand, Mr. Z. I think this is important. Psychoanalysis was created by a Jew and its first hearings were Jewish. Now these Jews were mostly secular Jews (Freud did write *The Interpretation of Dreams* in *Shul*). Being a Jew had to do with a commitment to humanistic values, the Enlightenment. Humanism and the intellect were the central aspects of Freud's Jewish identity. When he left Vienna and disbanded the Vienna Psychoanalytic Society, he said he was reminded of what the Jews did after the destruction of the Second Temple. Rabbi Johanan ben Zakkai went to Yavna and founded an academy, which is interesting because of what they studied at that academy. Of course, they studied the Tanakh at that academy. So here is Freud, the godless Jew, celebrating Johanan ben Zakkai, who was anything but a godless Jew. But I think the importance of how psychoanalysis developed a relation to humanistic values and the value of the intellect is a very important part and should be a part of the identity of an analyst. This is a part of my identity as a psychoanalyst.

Were you involved in the Jewish thinking? I mean, you were going to Yiddish schools from your childhood.

I was a secular Jew. My father was an atheist who went to the movies on Yom Kippur so he could drive my mother crazy because she was from an orthodox family. Then, of course, I became orthodox myself, maybe that involved some kind of connection in the relationship to my mother. But in college it changed dramatically. I went to Quaker meetings and worked for the United Farm Service Committee and disconnected myself from being Jewish. In medical school I was too busy for religion. In Topeka we sent out our children to Sunday school at the local congregation. We wanted to invite Harry Golden, editor of the Carolina Israelite to speak about integration. The rabbi was not very happy about it. He thought the local folk would say "Oh yes, do you wanna bring all your n****r friends?" It was only when I came back to New York that I joined the Synagogue so our son could get Bar Mitzvah. Then I got involved in YIVO.

That was central for you.

Yes, that became central for me. I organized a conference on anti-Semitism: "Old Demons New Debates: Anti-Semitism in the West", and one on the Jewish World of Sigmund Freud at YIVO. We were responsible for the Yiddish revival in New York. I organized the first New York Yiddish Film

Festival in 1972 and the second one in 1973. I brought together several institutions: YIVO, the Jewish Museum, the American Jewish Congress, the Workmen Circle, the 92nd Street Y. That, in itself, was an accomplishment. I learned a lot from bringing groups together, which I also did at the PEP CD-ROM symposiums. YIVO was responsible for the *klezmer* revival. The people that worked for us mined our extensive collection of *klezmer* sheet music.

What about anti-Semitism? I think there is a revival again.

Of course, there is. When Freud's father told him about the hat in the gutter incident, he was eleven years old. The incident happened before Freud was born. It was a more anti-Semitic time. The decade of 1860 was a much better time for the Jews, his father in telling the story about the hat knocked off his head was saying how much better things are now for Jews. For Freud it meant his father was a coward.

In the 1870s there was a big bank failure just as happened in the United States recently. A lot of banks failed because of the cheap imports from the United States and a housing bubble. Of course, the Jews were blamed. Around this time, the pogroms in Eastern Europe began – in 1880s. Anti-Semitism was really on the rise. Lueger, an anti-Semite, was elected mayor of Vienna. Jews became less hopeful about becoming part of society. It wasn't going to work. How did this impact on Freud? James Cuddihy wrote a book, *The Ordeal of Civility*. His thesis is that one of the things that Freud was doing by talking about the unconscious as universal, was affirming that the Gentiles are just as *shmutsik* as us. Freud's generation had a problem with their identification and connection with their fathers and their wish to become part of a society and part of the Enlightenment. What they did, in my opinion, was to become introspective and more self-aware about what was going on. I think that this is part of the whole ethos of psychoanalysis. During this period in the Habsburg empire there were two sciences that were established by Jews, one was psychoanalysis and the other was sociology. The people who started sociology were all or almost all Hapsburg Jews. I think the idea is the same. Sociology is an effort to understand oneself and how this has an impact on the culture.

Why did you get interested in YIVO?

I am very interested in history. Interest in YIVO, in Yiddish, and in Judaism, connect with my interest in history. I've also been interested in and written about the history of the American Psychoanalytic Association. I comment that it seemed strange that we as psychoanalysts are so interested in the history of our patients but have little interest in the history of our own institutions. How do we account for that?

You tell me.

Denial, avoidance, repression. A need not to know. It's easier to think about the history of our own patients than to think about our own history.

But for psychoanalysis that sounds dramatic. I was reading a paper by Ricardo Steiner on how terrible Ernest Jones, and even Freud, behaved with religion, with Vienna and Berlin societies.

On what specifically?

Actually, they were negotiating with Goring.

Oh, yes, yes.

And accepting the exclusion of Jews by those societies.

The one who was admirable in that regard was Richard Sterba, who wasn't Jewish. He said if the Jews go, he would leave as well. He is Bob Michels' father-in-law.

No!

You didn't know that?

No. no, no… I think there are so many things that we don't like to know about our origins as analysts that actually somehow have chosen our behavior, but there are some exceptions in New York psychoanalytic wars.

That was written by Doug Kirsner in his book *Unfree Associations*. He got a lot of it from me. But this connects with the more general principle about psychoanalysis and the attitude of the elite. The idea that patients certainly shouldn't know about bad stuff in relation to Freud or anyone else because that would disturb the transference and would affect the treatment. I think there is something about hiding bad things and hiding secrets from yourself and the community and the patient…

And they are rationalizing. I'm not telling you the truth because you can be damaged …

Exactly, exactly. As if they are protecting psychoanalysis, right? But they are protecting their own position, their own standing, their own posture in the field, rather than really protecting psychoanalysis. If we are going to have any standing in the scientific and academic arena, we have to tell the truth. We can't have secrets. One of the big complaints about how institutes run is the lack of transparency, so people can't say what they think because maybe a candidate may hear what they're saying, and this would affect the analysis. I think they believe that, but I think that comes out of insecurity and fear.

But we are talking about anti-Semitism being a big sword of Damocles hanging over every Jew, and that's how secure you feel. Suddenly, you might feel Vienna: half of the physicians were Jews and the lawyers were Jews. What can happen to you? And then it does. This is a big era of anti-Semitism, again. Something that nobody thought might occur again and then it happened.

Let me get back to what was happening in Vienna. At that time the Jews were very successful. Freud himself and other Jews thought that the cause of anti-Semitism was the unwashed, *unkempt shtetl* Jews who came from the *shtetl* and were very much present in Vienna. That is what was causing anti-Semitism. I think that was a rationalization. I think it was the Gentile envy of the success of the Jews. It was the successful Jews that generated anti-Semitism rather than feelings about the poor Jews. I am convinced that Freud was very embarrassed, ashamed of his *shtetl* Galician origins. He made the point that his parents or grandparents came originally from Western Germany, Hamburg. He had a family romance about his origins. He didn't want to locate his family in Galicia. That's what he said. There was an article in Haaretz in the late '30s by someone named Grinberg. He traveled to Vienna from Buchach and gave a paper about a play "Yochanan The Prophet, a *shtetl* Jew" where he quotes Freud saying, "I would rather be the Jew in the tuxedo than the Jew in the koftin". I think Freud was very sensitive and embarrassed about his *shtetl* origins, when it impeded his efforts to assimilate. On the other hand, he was very proud of being a Jew in his own terms. He said, "I used to be a German, my language was German, my culture was German, but because of anti-Semitism, I am a Jew." I think now, Jews say it's really not because of us but because of the Israelis. They do not recognize that anti-Semitism comes not from Israel, but from the same roots that anti-Semitism has come from for two thousand years.

Which are...? I've just read My Unwritten Books by George Steiner. He is a secular Jew...

I've heard about it.

He says the main cause of anti-Semitism is that we have killed God. But, first, how can you kill God? And second, if we had killed God that is why Christianity exists. So, they hate us not because we have killed God but because we had given them a God.

That's exactly the point. The problem is that Christianity and Islam are derivatives of Judaism and Abrahamaic traditions that came from Judaism. That's why Christians have to kill us. That is why the Muslims have to get rid of us as well.

There is an extra bit for your excitement. Steiner says that we have given them such a terrible God that they are right to hate that God. The problem is that instead of hating God and denying it, they accept that God and they hate the people who have given them that God.

That's all about the same thing.

But what sort of a hate. I'm thinking in the Venezuelan president Chavez and his association with the Iranians. I think there is a real risk that I feel.

Of course! But what happened to Castro? He must've had some sort of connection with Jews who came early from Europe in his earlier life. All of a sudden, he was saying nice things about Israel.

About Jews, but he is also now changing his mind about homosexuality because in the beginning they persecuted homosexuals.

And now he's not?

Now he says that it was a mistake… You were saying that an important part of your involvement with Jewish issues derives from your interest in history…

It is also my connection to my parents, to my family who came from Eastern Europe and my father who came from Podolia. I wrote an article for the YIVO Encyclopedia on psychoanalysis in Eastern Europe, an article about Jews in American Psychoanalysis, which is in the Encyclopedia of American Jews and an article in Encyclopedia Britannica —the health and science issue — which is entitled "Psychoanalysis Burgeoning and Beleaguered." It was written in the '80s. My wife tells me that when I go to a dinner party the first things I ask are, "Where are you from? Where were your parents from? Where were your grandparents from?" The idea that Moses was an Egyptian was Freud's origination myth for the Jewish people. The myth is that he really wasn't originally Jewish, but he was Egyptian. It is part of his family romance as a Jew in Habsburg Vienna.

And a prince, because he was not a humble Jew, he was really a prince.

Right. He wanted to be the son of Hannibal and his father would not be who he was.

Yes, and the Jewish general Napoleon who was not Jewish, but he thought he was.

He thought he was. You know why Freud's father left Freiburg?

I think he didn't do well there.

Yes, but do you know why the business failed? Because the train did not stop anymore at Freiburg. They changed the station. What if they hadn't changed the station and he had stayed in Freiburg? What would Freud have become? A wool manufacturer? A factory manager?

Or if he had emigrated with his relatives to England and become a very rich man. What about his grandson? He is one of the top painters in the world.

Incredible.

18 to 19 million dollars per picture.

But he has a lot of problems. He's a gambler apparently but he buys a lot of houses.

What about being married to an analyst? What about Arlene's process?

That's a very important question. We got married when I was finishing college on the first day in spring, March 21, 1954. Then I started medical school. Arlene who was also a graduate of the University of Chicago worked to support us for the four years in medical school and all she had was a BA. She gave up pursuing a career at that time. I always had the wish that somehow Arlene would also have a successful career, and when she did, I had the wish that she should belong to every organization I belonged to. That was why I became involved in the lawsuit, which is a whole other story. When I was in medical school, she taught at a public school. During my stint in Petersburg she taught Remedial Reading at Richard Bland College. She began treating children and adolescents with learning disabilities. When we moved to New York for my analytic training, she started an Ed.D. at Teachers College. She took mostly statistics courses because in clinical or theoretical psychology courses she was identified as the wife of a Freudian. Her instructors would ask her, "What would Freud say about that?". Her thesis was on language acquisition in 6-year-olds (our youngest daughter was 6 years old). She got her Ed.D. and she applied to the NYPSI as a research candidate. She brought all her research data to the interview. I'm sure David

Kairys and John McDevitt had no idea what it was about; they asked her if she was interested in practice. She said, "Yes" and wasn't accepted. Arlene has never gone to an Institute. She has had no formal training. It is like being home-schooled. You know that?

No.

She is an autodidact. She couldn't get into an institute, so she decided to train on her own. She went into analysis with Jack Arlow, she paid for supervision, she got a group of people who met with George Gross, read all of Freud, and took other courses. She was in supervision with Donald Kaplan who was running for president at the Freudian Society against Emily Anne Gargiulo. He said, "Do me a favor, join the Freudian Society, and vote for me". She joined the Freudian Society and after she became a member, she became involved in the lawsuit and I did, as well. When the lawsuit was settled, she became a member of the IPA, IPTAR and APsaA. That is how she became an *echt* psychoanalyst. We have always shared offices. We practice together where we live. Her *hegira* is an interesting story. I think she has been much better for not having formal institute training.

So, she must have been one of the very few cases of an analyst who has become an analyst through alternative routes.

Correct. I don't think there are that many but clearly she was a very determined person and I was determined.

And how did you feel in those days? You were a member of NYPSI when she was not accepted.

Well, I wasn't very happy about it. I thought that it was totally stupid.

How active was she in the lawsuit and you as well?

There was a meeting of Division 39 in Puerto Rico to organize the lawsuit. I remember the group: Arlene, Ernie Lawrence, Rita Frankiel, Nat Stockhammer. Someone turns to me and says, "What are you doing here? Aren't you a member of The American Psychoanalytic Association?" "Of course," I said. And then they said: "Are you a spy for Herb Schlessinger?" Herb was a member of the American and not that sympathetic with the lawsuit. We gave lot of money to the lawsuit. Money made the difference.

How did it come about? It was clear to the psychologists that the whole thing was unfair. There were several motivations. Some had misgivings about winning the lawsuit because they wondered what impact this would have on their own institutes. APsaA was preventing their members from teaching and supervising in non-medical institutes. That could be construed as restraint of trade. Some felt that they should pursue the suit with the hope that it would bankrupt APsaA. So, there were three different attitudes: some felt they shouldn't sue, some felt they should sue because it would open up training, and some had a 'burn the house down' attitude. They got Bryant Welch. He was a psychoanalyst and a lawyer.

There were four people in the suit Arnie Schneider, Bryant Welch, Helen Desmond and Toni Bernay. There was a meeting with Ed Joseph, President of the APsaA in Washington to work out a settlement. After the meeting Joseph sent Division 39 a bill for his dry cleaning. The plaintiffs thought this was the ultimate arrogance. Joseph said it was a mistake. Then Dick Simons became president. Dick was terrific. The smoking gun was that Ed Joseph said in some public meeting that this really was a pocketbook issue. We can't let you win because it would affect our livelihood. The lawyer from Paul Weiss argued our request for summary judgment and lost. Jack Arlow and I felt that we were very poorly represented. The lawyer that APsaA used was the lawyer NYPSI used. I got a call from Fred Pine, who said that they were going to file an anti-trust action. I told this to Helen Fisher who told this to Dick Simons and they agreed that they needed another lawyer. Dick Simon had met Joel Klein at a meeting at the American Psychiatric Association. He hired Joe Klein. That made all the difference because Joel Klein was determined to settle the lawsuit. Kaplan, the lawyer from Paul Weiss, said we could win but Klein said no way. Dick thought we shouldn't win and, in the end, losing the lawsuit saved the APsaA.

What did you feel at the time?

I was all for settling the lawsuit. My only reservation was we should train psychologists but shouldn't be forced to do it. But the fact is that if they hadn't had a lawsuit, we would still be deliberating.

What about living with a psychoanalyst or being a psychoanalytic couple?

I feel incredibly lucky, fortunate to have this kind of relationship. There's so much that we can do together and share. I joined the Freudian Society, I belong to the American Psychological Association, I belong to Division 39, both of us belong to all those organizations together. You know she doesn't belong to the NYPSI or TPI or NYU but we both belong to the Psychoanalytic Association of New York (PANY). We go to meetings together so that gives us many opportunities for a certain kind of connection. Arlene writes her things and I write my things, but we also collaborate. We've written things together. We wrote a very interesting paper about gambling and three Las Vegas movies: *Leaving Las Vegas, Bugsy,* and *Casino*. It was published several years ago. We wrote a paper together on the relationship between psychoanalytic theory and psychoanalytic technique. We used a case of Arlene's. We had responses from Self psychologists, Kleinians, Relationalists, and others. They responded and then we responded to the responses. It's a very good paper. It is published in the journal of the NYPSI, which is now defunct. We are going to present the paper in Mexico City [IPA Congress 2011] and respond to candidates' presentations from three institutes.

What comes to my mind is that actually all of the 39, the lawsuit and everything else was also a fight of Arlene to join you.

That's correct. You're absolutely correct.

In a way she wanted to be legitimate, to become your true wife, your mate, not a sort of professional mistress. She wanted to be your professional wife.

That's right because this gives us a kind of equal footing and equal status. We both see patients, we both practice very similarly, we go to meetings together we write together. What more can we want, from a relationship? Not many people have that advantage, have that luxury, which it certainly is. Socially I am more involved with her friends, I'm more connected with her groups than I am with my own.

Why? How come?

Because most of the people that I know belong to the Freudian Society and IPTAR. I'm not that socially involved with the people at the NYPSI because they see me as the maverick, the loose cannon or whatever. I used to belong to CAPS, The Center for Advanced Psychoanalytic Studies in Princeton. It is another organization that perpetuates the elitism of the APsaA. I wanted to present the Mexico paper at CAPS with Arlene, but they refused because she wasn't a member of the group. I ended up resigning from the group. I think on some level there was a certain amount of hostility toward Arlene, perhaps because of the lawsuit.

Did they see you as a traitor?

You know what? My friends excuse it by saying, "Well you were just doing it for your wife. So that wasn't so bad. You really didn't believe it, but you are doing it for your wife". Do you follow that?

Yes, yes.

And the same thing with the certification thing. Some said: "The only reason you're doing this is because of your wife". The group does not tolerate dissidence. They have a fixed point of view and dismiss or deny contradictions.

Is APsaA now accepting psychologists?

They certainly accept psychologists and I don't think there's any discrimination at all but it's curious because some of the non-medical people are becoming even more conservative and supportive of the BoPS exclusionary principles. Perhaps it is identification with the aggressor.

It is because they have become part of the elite.

Right, I won't mention names but there are people I can think of along those lines.

What about your children in terms of having a mother and father who are psychoanalysts?

I think children of psychoanalysts are very wary about psychoanalysis. I think all of our children have been in treatment of one kind or another and have their own issues. I was just having a conversation with our daughter today about the trip to Mexico and I was very pleased that she was interested. I'm very reluctant to tell the kids about what I'm doing.

How many kids do you have?

We have three children, two grandchildren.

What do they do?

Rebecca was a labor and delivery nurse. She divorced and then became a nurse educator. She is in San Francisco. Steven was a public defender in Chicago, he worked for the County and did death penalty defense. It's very interesting because he wrote the brief that Governor Ryan used to commute the sentences of 188 prisoners on death row. I said to Steven, "I haven't saved 188 people in my life". He wanted to become the head of the whole Public Defender Department, but he didn't get the job. The person who got the job fired him, which is not unusual, right? So, he went into private practice. He is doing very well. Last week he won his first jury trial and he is doing phenomenally financially.

A blessing in disguise.

A blessing in disguise. He went to the University of Chicago. He has an interesting career. He went to graduate school in history at the University of Rochester to work with Eugene Genevese, but Genevese had left for London so he spent a year working for Christopher Lasch and then left Graduate School. He worked for three years as a waiter in a Chinese restaurant, taught himself Chinese and read all of Freud. Then he went to law school, Brooklyn Law. After he finished law school, he decided he didn't want to work for a law firm. He applied to 104 programs for teaching Legal Writing and Legal Reasoning. He got one job, at Kent IT in Chicago. Steven is an incredibly inner-directed person, not like anyone I have ever known. After that he clerked for [William G.] Clark, Chief Justice of the Illinois Supreme Court. Then he became a public defender. He has had visible cases, including the Brown's Chicken massacre. All of our kids are interested in doing good.

Don't you feel disappointed that none of them has followed you?

I am not sure. They have their own life and their own interests. I'm very impressed with the good stuff they do. Our other daughter, she and her husband are in a way very important people in psychoanalysis. They manage many of the analytic meetings in NYC. They run my book publishing company, and they run the blog. Frankly, I couldn't do what I do without them. Do you have an assistant?

Yes, Dana, and without her I certainly wouldn't be able to do anything... I have two children, a daughter and a son. My son works with computers, my daughter is an architect. As there aren't psychoanalysts in my family, I decided to give my 40 years collection of psychiatric and psychoanalytic journals to a university in Lima, some thousand psychiatric books to the Peruvian Psychiatric Association and all my child stuff to the Peruvian Children Psychotherapy Association. I kept the books I use, but all the rest I have already distributed.

We sent ours to China because there's nobody in New York I could give that stuff to.

I decided to do that, but I think if one of my children would be an analyst, obviously I would give it all to them.

I don't know any three individuals like my children who have as good a sibling relationship with each other. Tamar and [her husband] Larry spend one day of the week at a soup kitchen for the homeless, they volunteer. I would say there is something *lamid vodnik* about them. Do you know the term?

No.

Lamid vodnik means "stands for 36". There were 36 good people in the world. *The Last of the Just* by Andre Schwarz-Bart?

Yes.

That's a *lamid vodnik*. It's an especially good person. So, I've just made up a new word, it's an adjective. That's a good word, it talks about someone who has a genuine feeling of humanity for other people.

That was after or before your choice of profession?

Much, much, after. It's very complicated. My father was murdered.

How come?

Well, he was in business, he had a painting and decorating company. Someone at his work knew he had the payroll. It was the day before the Fourth of July: "Your money or your life". He was stabbed and died. My father was the kind of person who would fight. He told me that when he was in Palestine, he would walk across the Galilee even though he knew it was dangerous. He had a brother, David, my middle name, who was two years younger and wanted to join the Army as well. My father told his father it was too dangerous. They came to his town looking for him and they found this brother apparently wearing his hat and they killed him. I'm sure my father had a profound sense of guilt so when he wanted to stay in Russia his father told him he should leave and try to get his family out of Russia. He came to the United States, he worked very hard, he got a visa and money for his sister to come. But just as he had the money, they closed immigration. His sister couldn't come. He sent the money and the visa to his cousin who came as his sister to Canada. She was a Yiddish reader. She had two children, one died. The other is a physician. There's an annual lecture in Montreal in her honor. My father's sisters were killed in the Holocaust, his brother went to Brazil. The other brother stayed, was in the Russian Army and we learned recently that he was a General and was killed in the Battle for Berlin. The only thing that puzzles me is how could a Jew from the cohort of the '20s survive the Stalin purges in 1936. But apparently, he was still alive in 1945. Moises, every Jew has a story.

That's why so many Jews are novelists.

That's right.

And others are psychoanalysts… But your father was killed…

In 1976. He was murdered.

What a waste! And you think it was because he wanted to fight.

I think so. But to what extent he was influenced by the guilt about his brother's death?

How did that affect you?

It was very traumatic.

Because, of course, it was a death that in a way was avoidable.

To me it was a terrible thing. They found the person who did it, they convicted him, they put him in Rikers Island prison and he escaped. He went to Florida, got married, started a family and a new life for a while. The detectives in Borough Park, who are very protective of the community, finally tracked him down in Florida. He was brought back to New York.

A film maker, Barbara Kopple, who did "Harlan County" wanted to do a documentary about his rehabilitation. I felt this would be terribly traumatic for my mother. We threatened to sue, and she dropped the project.

He went back to prison?

Yes. And she didn't make a movie about him.

You have terrible stories about your family. The eldest sister of my mother, there were six, came to New York. She was a dressmaker and her husband worked in a laundry. They had a daughter who is still alive. She did send money to bring her siblings, but immigration was closed by then. That's why my mother and two other sisters and brother went to Peru.

So you have family in the United States.

I have first cousins and quite a lot of Malamuds (my mother's last name). My father's immigration was earlier, so I have family in the USA and Argentina as you have in Brazil. Something that interests me is how much of a Jew I am, but also how much of a Peruvian I am, how much a typical representative of a Latin-American Jew I am.

I think I am unlike a lot of colleagues, because I enjoy connecting with people all over the world on the basis of my being Jewish and on the basis of Yiddish and family. I think that's unusual.

What about the other American psychoanalytic Jews?

I know very few colleagues who are quite like me. Selma Duckler, from the American Psychoanalytic Foundation, was at a meeting at Sandy Abend's.

His wife Carol said to her, "You're gonna meet Arnie Richards, he's probably the most Jewish psychoanalyst there is".

As a compliment?

I don't know. I'm often faulted. I mean, some people fault the blog because it is too Jewish.

What do you understand they mean by that?

I think it has to do with their wish to be more disconnected from being Jewish and to insist that this is not very important to them. I think very few people have the same Yiddish background as I do. Sometimes I make a joke, "I'm involved in lost causes, psychoanalysis and Yiddish".

When you finished your job as editor of JAPA you remained with the taste for editing and applied for editor of the International Journal of Psychoanalysis. I think it might have been a blessing in disguise that you didn't get the job and started your website.

I have to admit that I was ambivalent about becoming editor of the International Journal, but I really thought I could make a difference in terms of the internet and so forth, it certainly seemed to me to be a challenge. I probably understood that I wouldn't get the job.

They wanted another editor, an American editor to claim that the International Journal is international, but it is not international.

I think the relationship between the Executive Council of the British Society and the Journal is very different from the relationship between APsaA Executive Council and JAPA. At JAPA I felt I had total control, I didn't have to account to anybody, really nobody told me what I couldn't do or couldn't print. I had total autonomy and independence and I value that very much.

How do you organize your blog? How does it function?

What I can tell you is that I find everything for the blog. Every morning I search the web and find things that are related to psychoanalysis, Freud, or whatever and I send it to Lawrence Schwartz Partners and they post it. I get great contributions: original novels, original plays, ideas. I have a very large editorial board from all over the world but essentially, Moises, it is just me. When I was editor of JAPA I felt I had an audience, I have a need to communicate with —if not the world— with the psychoanalytic world. I probably post more on websites than anybody else. Maybe it's some kind of social need I have; I want to engage people in a dialogue to raise their cultural and intellectual awareness. That's what it's about. I think to me it is a wonderful opportunity, to connect people. And I think technology is the future. Journals are not the future. It's to make stuff accessible for everybody.

What about peer review? Some people are very much against it, others think it's essential.

You put something on the web and the peer review becomes everybody. All can comment and propose changes. The web has unlimited space. In a journal, space is limited; you can only publish papers of a certain size, with a certain number of words. The web provides for the rapid dissemination of information.

Let's talk about who influenced your thinking.

For the last ten years, or so, I've been influenced by a Polish immunologist and philosopher of science, Ludwig Fleck, who in 1936 wrote a book on the origin and development of scientific knowledge. Fleck believes that science is influenced by personal, psychological, cultural, social, and historical factors. He developed the idea of the Denk [thought] collective, and the 'thought style' – people with similar ideas formed groups. In APsaA, BoPS is one "thought collective" and the ordinary members is another. He called it "the sociology of scientific knowledge". I proposed "the sociology of psychoanalytic knowledge". You cannot understand a person's psychoanalytic position without understanding the facts that impact on its development, as is true for all sciences.

What about American psychoanalytic thinking?

There are different collectives and sub-collectives. I certainly was influenced by Charlie Brenner and Jack Arlow. The centrality of conflict and unconscious fantasy were foundational to them, but they also had their differences. Brenner, as I anticipated early on in my introduction to his Festschrift that I edited with Marty Willick, held views that were in step with the anti-metapsychology developed in response to David Rapaport by George Klein, and Merton Gill and Roy Schafer. They were against the concept of reified agencies Id, Ego, and Superego. Charlie didn't appreciate my telling him his ideas were like Roy's and Roy didn't like the idea that his idea was like Charlie's. Jack Arlow didn't go as far as Charlie, but he said that the Id, the Ego, and Superego only existed in psychoanalytic textbooks, not in a person's mind. I was interested in the anti-nosological approach, which was central to Karl Menninger and the anti-metapsychological approach also had its roots in Topeka.

My supervisors were also important influences. Ted Lipin, who no one could understand (like Lacan perhaps), was important. He stressed looking to the moment to moment variations in the patient's productions. First you pay attention to slips, elisions, contradictions, double meanings, metaphors (like Lacan) and then step back to formulate the overriding organizing of unconscious fantasy. In the paper that Arlene and I wrote about theory and technique, we came to the conclusion that people that were closest to us because of the centrality of conflict in unconscious fantasy were the Arlow-Brennarians and the Kleinians.

Then there is the Richards and Richards theory of psychoanalytic technique. This is a joint project. Our theory is that a theoretician develops a theory of technique to counter his or her own anti-therapeutic proclivities. For example, Sigmund Freud was a busy body and activist. He was always intrusive on his patients' lives. He told them to get married and so he stressed abstinence. Otto Fenichel was an incredibly obsessional human being. He kept the record of every postcard and every playbill. His stress was on affect. Heinz Kohut, who is probably one of the most narcissistic human beings, stressed empathy. Kurt Eissler, was an activist who would call his patients in the middle of the night because he forgot to tell them something, writes about parameters. Paul Gray, who many experienced as an authoritarian person, writes about the superego. Jack Arlow is very intuitive, he can listen to one session or half a session and formulate the operative unconscious fantasy, stresses waiting for the evidence. Charles Brenner is one of the most thoughtful, kind and generous people I know. He's always the first to offer condolences, but he writes, when there is a death in your patient's family don't say you are sorry.

And you?

I also am an activist and a revolutionary, so I stress analytic restraint. Todd Essig, a relationalist, told me that relational psychoanalysts are those who had trouble getting dates in high school.

I think in general lots of analysts I know are or were very bad at dating.

So, is there anything we can say about Winnicott according to my theory? What was his central therapeutic idea? The holding environment?

Yes, the holding environment. He was a transgressor.

Yes. What about Bion?

What do you think about that sort of British School that in a sense had produced a very peculiar theory?

I think my problem with them is they generate acolytes rather than serious conversation as far as I can tell. I think the British tend to be quite unaccepting of difference and I was told that before you can publish a paper you had to get an imprimatur from Betty Joseph or Hanna Segal. Is that really so?

It used to be. While I was training there, if you were from one group — that was my case — one supervisor had to be from my group, but I could choose a supervisor from another group, which was my case, and my second supervisor was Nina Coltart. But the Kleinians were the group that had to be supervised by Kleinians only.

I may give the Kleinians more credit than they deserve. I'm sympathetic to their centrality of conflicts and unconscious fantasy, but I think they talk a lot in the session and impose their view on the patient... They talk too much.

Do you know the story about the difference between the Kleinians and Freudians? In a Freudian analysis the analyst might die, and the patient will barely know and in a Kleinian analysis the patient might die, and the analyst won't know.

Oh, that's wonderful! I value precision in language. I don't like what people say in ten sentences what they could say in one. People complain about me, they say my communications are too cryptic. I think I probably talk more in a conversation than when I write.

What about French psychoanalysis? Does it interest you?

We are publishing the complete work of Jean Laplanche in English translated from the French. Look, I don't speak French, I don't understand French and I think, probably in that sense, I am pretty narrow in regard to my focus on American Psychoanalysis, self-psychology, object relations, relational psychoanalysis. I am not as knowledgeable about either the Brits or the French.

With whom do you feel you are speaking with the same voice?

Warren Poland, he's one of my closest friends. Another very close friend is Arnie Wilson, who is a psychologist. I used to be very close to Bill Grossman before he died. Obviously, I've been close to Jack and to Charlie. Then, I am close to people that are not members of the APsaA, Shelly Bach, Steve Ellman, and my co-authors, Art Lynch and Janet Bachant.

Steve Ellman is very much into research.

His research is physiological research, but he is interested in psychoanalytic theory. Have you seen his book?

Yes.

It's about this thing.

But at the beginning…

That was in a different kind of research. It has dealt with dreams, it was neurophysiological research, it is not the kind of research that is really analytic, in my opinion. I think one of the problems with research is that it is under a committee. It's an opportunity to give up money.

You become a paid...

I always felt that some people want to become president so they can reward their friends and punish their enemies. That's one thing I tried not to do as editor of JAPA. The other thing I didn't do is, what some other editors have done, insisting that every paper that gets published has you as a reference. If you look at one issue of the Quarterly, every paper had Harry Smith (aka Henry Smith) as a reference, we went through them all.

What is the destiny of publications?

That's a good question. I'm supposed to write an article as the former editor of JAPA. The Division 39 Journal edited by Joe Reppen was a good journal, he was succeeded by Elliot Jurist and it's not nearly as good now. I have published several papers in the *Psychoanalytic Review*. I think Harry Smith overall did a pretty good job at the Quarterly, except for his not rejecting papers. I think there is an issue with print journal publication because unless they're subsidized by the organization, the publisher makes money now, by selling individual papers online. They may charge $30 for the PDF of a single paper. I am not sure that APsaA is benefiting from this. The publisher can get as much from selling three papers than from a single subscription and there is no postage or printing cost. That's a new model!

What is more of concern is book publishing because psychoanalytic book publishing is becoming a disaster. You're lucky if you can get five hundred books published and make money. It is a big problem, and that's why I started IPBooks.

How many copies do you usually print? A thousand copies?

A very few books sell a thousand copies now.

Is it because people don't read? Is it because there are less people interested?

First of all, you know that many publishers are no longer publishing psychoanalytic books anymore. Several analytic presses are out of the business because they feel they can't make a living.

Karnac is the only one.

Yes, Karnac is OK. The internet is also a factor. People read stuff. Maybe Kindle will help. *Freud Jewish World* [Full title - *The Jewish World of Sigmund Freud: Essays on Cultural Roots and the Problems of Religious Identity*] is on Kindle now. We sent 50 copies to Mexico and sold them all. But that's a crossover book that appeals to analysts and Jews. Once upon a time, Charlie Brenner's elementary textbook sold a million copies over the years.

Some Lacanians do sell a lot.

Yes, that's true. That's a whole other phenomenon.

Do you have an opinion on that?

On what?

On Lacanians.

Do you know the joke when you meet a Lacanian?

No.

He makes you an offer you can't understand.

But they're really successful.

Yes, and are getting more successful.

They have cornered the academic market in many European countries.

Right. And what about Argentina?

What has happened in Argentina is that the societies have incorporated Lacanians. The only thing is that they should keep more or less the time schedules and give full sessions. Some Lacanians have accepted that. There is a very strong Lacanian influence on some of the Argentinean Societies.

Lacanians understand that life is theatre and people like to go to the theatre.

Perhaps we should learn something from them.

Yes, but you have to be willing to put yourself out there and try to connect. I've always thought a lot of Foucault.

He was a good friend of psychoanalysis.

I like Foucault, and I can understand him, I understand what he wrote. The problem is that Lacanians are less understandable.

What do you feel is ahead of you?

My practice, I have to spend half my time in clinical work. That's bread and butter, the day to day stimulation and challenge of helping people.

How many sessions a week?

About 25 a week. I have some patients four times a week, three times a week, two times a week, one time a week.

You were saying that they are the same type of patients you've always had.

People have interpersonal problems, marital problems, depression and anxiety, and so forth.

Returning to the blog, I have the blog but what I do hope is that this publishing venture can serve a very real need for the psychoanalytic community and that I can publish books and get them distributed. I think that will be a real contribution.

Are you still involved in your society?

I'm currently involved in the APsaA because we are doing a letter in support of a by-law amendment, but I'm not very involved in my own society at all. My latest project was that they wanted to fire the person who runs the bookstore, Richard, so they could save money and give more money to the administrator. They came to me to see if I can help because they felt the bookstore was very important, so I got my friend Silvia Brody to contribute with some 7000 dollars for his salary in return for them naming the bookstore, the Sylvia Brody Bookstore and putting a plaque on the outside of the building. They were very reluctant to do it but as you know or may not know, I got someone to give a million dollars to establish the Bernard Pacella Parent Child Center of NYPSI. There is a plaque on the outside of the building for them. This came through a patient of Bernard Pacella who wanted to give this money for something connected with children. I came up with that idea. A million dollars is a lot of money, so I was very pleased about doing that.

You have been involved in the Sigourney Prize also.

From the very beginning.

It is the most important psychoanalytic prize.

Absolutely. But they should rethink who should be getting it. Should it be going to younger people to use, to build their careers, and to tell people to recognize their careers? I don't know.

That is a good question… Well, it has been a pleasure having this long talk with you.

Thank you very much.

1920 Haifa. Arnie's father, Schmuel Ironi née Gurodovich (Urbnanite)
1st from the right in front, with his work group

Sigmund Freud's Death
Announced in the Yiddish *Forward*

Karl Menninger and Eleanor Roosevelt

Charles Brenner, Arnold Richards, & Jacob Arlow

Arnold Richards and Arlene Kramer Richards in Ningbo, China

Arnie Richards with Wuhan, China Class

Wuhan, China Faculty

Arnold Richards's Afterword

I see the almost full decade that has elapsed since the interviews with Moises Lemlij as a time of consolidation of my professional, clinical, and pedagogic identity. Since the interviews were conducted, I have remained very active professionally in CFS and AIP. I have taught at both institutes, and am a TA in AIP. The opportunity to connect with candidates, who are our future, is very important to me.

I have also written and published many psychoanalytic papers and reviews over the past decade. I have contributed to many journals. And I have also published new work in the volumes of my selected papers. Of these selected papers, volumes I and II have already been published and translated into Chinese. Volume III is in production and Volume IV is in preparation. All four volumes are edited by Arthur Lynch, and have introductions also written by him. I think there will be enough contributions for a fifth volume within the next two years.

Eight years ago Arlene Kramer Richards and I started a psychoanalytic psychotherapy training program in Wuhan, China. We have already completed two three-year sessions, with more than 200 students meeting twice per year. In 2020 we will conclude the third course, four sessions in three years. The institute includes faculty from China, France, Greece, Turkey, Argentina, and Israel, under the leadership of Dr. Tong, a Chinese psychologist who is now an IPA training analyst. Many of the faculty were recruited by Arlene and me. All the faculty give lectures to all the students and there is often a daily three-hour supervisory meeting with a smaller group (20 to 30 attendees). In addition to meeting in person in Wuhan, many of the faculty also conduct supervisory and didactic sessions on the internet.

I completed last year a course on 50 essential papers in psychoanalysis, attended by more than three hundred mental health professionals. I also offered a single online supervision exercise via Skype for Chinese speakers worldwide that was attended by 38,000.

A recent personal and professional consolidation of mine has been my work as a book publisher. IPBooks was established in 2007. Since then it has published more than 140 books. In addition to books on psychoanalysis, and psychoanalytic literary and film criticism, IPBooks has published works of fiction, poetry, humor, children's books and memoirs. Our books are widely distributed. They are available on Amazon and are sold at major psychoanalytic meetings.

Many IPBooks have been reviewed in prestigious journals, including *The Journal of the American Psychoanalytic Association,* and *Psychoanalytic Quarterly. The Interwoven Lives of Sigmund, Anna and W. Ernest Freud* by Daniel Benveniste was reviewed by *the Times Literary Supplement,* probably the most important English language book review publication. Of course, without the IPBooks staff, including especially Larry Schwartz and Tamar Schwartz, I would not have been able to accomplish much.

Finally there is a larger context for my professional life. A central figure for me is the philosopher of science who formulated the concept of the thought collective, Ludwik Fleck. His insights have contributed to my work of offering critiques to help us all remain true to our core values and save us from ourselves. In addition to the psychoanalytic thought collective, I see myself as belonging to a Jewish left intellectual thought collective concerned with progressive values. With all my experience in China over the past decade, I now also have a more global perspective. And I will always be grateful to the colleagues and students I've met and worked with there for their generosity.

Estela Welldon

How did your interest in psychoanalysis begin?

I first began as a teacher and did a specialization in children with Down syndrome. Later I realized that I actually wanted to work on something broader to try to understand the human mind in context, and that also encompassed familial and social influences. I decided to enter the Faculty of Medicine of Mendoza [Argentina], which had been founded three or four years before, to study medicine and become a psychiatrist. I had no idea about psychoanalysis then, though I found out rather quickly. We were 60 students, half men and half women. This is a very important fact because since then I have never encountered prejudices against women.

In what year was this?

I don't really remember. I think it was at the end of Perón's government. It must have been around 1954 or 1955. The course of Psychiatry was taught by a Spaniard who was very adept at the biological perspective and opposed to the dynamic. Due to students' demands, the course of Medical Psychology was created, and Horacio Etchegoyen was appointed as professor. I believe he was the first psychoanalyst to leave Buenos Aires for the province, and also the first to enter the university as a professor. The situation was a little tense because we, the few students there, believed we were the owners of this new project. This is a very interesting fact because there were many problems of transference and countertransference in this kind of contract. For example, at the time I was a student, I was simultaneously in analysis with Professor Etchegoyen. This situation became even more complicated afterwards, because I won a teaching assistantship competition, so I also became his "employee". I remember that I was advised to go to Buenos Aires to see Enrique Racker, who had been Etchegoyen's analyst, and who was known for his work on transference and countertransference. His advice was very simple: that I move to another university. This was impossible advice, first, I could not change from one faculty to another because the curriculums of Buenos Aires and Mendoza were completely different. Secondly, I could not leave Mendoza because of practical personal problems. Finally, Racker told me that what I had to do was to continue my psychoanalysis with Etchegoyen in Mendoza and he warned me that it would be based almost exclusively on implicit and explicit conflicts in relation to transference and countertransference.

Some quite funny things happened. I had my sessions — five sessions a week — very early in the morning. Etchegoyen, who was very traditional and of absolute integrity, would shake your hand at the beginning and at the end of the session. Following the session, I would go to my job in the faculty and if I arrived five minutes late Etchegoyen would kick up an awful fuss. As a psychoanalyst he had been so kind half an hour before, but as soon as he became my superior again, he was angry about my unpunctuality. I remember this psychoanalytic experience with great affection and admiration. It was very enriching, despite all the things that could have contaminated the analysis. In addition, it was also the one that most aligned with the theoretical principles of psychoanalysis. This caught my attention once I arrived in London.

Mendoza was a totally conservative city and the arrival of Etchegoyen shocked everyone because at the time people associated psychoanalysis with child sexuality and sexual perversions. This scandal ended in a deplorable manner, almost like in medieval times of the Hammer of Witches, and in the end the "authorities" got him thrown out of the university despite all the student support.

Etchegoyen is a radical individual and not at all disposed to compromises. The truth is that when he was thrown out, the faculty was very shaken and there were very serious problems. This happened just as I was graduating as a doctor, very much supported by my analysis and all the experiences I had had in the Department of Medical Psychology. Our training was the most complete, and not only in psychoanalytic subjects. For example, we had the theoretical sessions on Wednesday night, where we would read and study all the works of Freud and Jaspers. Etchegoyen was the type of person who wanted to know about everything, in an almost obsessive way, that is, that we knew everything about biology, everything about psychology. Thanks to him we had a psychoanalytic training that was really first class. We also had prestigious guest lecturers from different areas and universities, like Enrique Pichon-Rivière, Carlos Alberto Seguín and Mimi Langer. All these people came, stayed for their respective semesters and then left. I was also supervised in Buenos Aires by Pichon-Rivière on group therapy. I had the privilege of presenting work together with Etchegoyen and Omar Lazarte, a Jungian psychotherapist. I was still a medical student, and it was at a psychoanalytic congress in Chile.

At this congress all the students stayed in the same residential "home" and in our talks after the sessions we could appreciate how the psychoanalysis students in Buenos Aires were divided into two groups: one pro-Pichon-Rivière and another pro-Rascovsky. They competed fiercely to determine who was the best of the two psychoanalysts. The favourite reference point to determine who was the best was who had had fewer suicides among the people they had analysed. I was speechless and grateful for the "luck" that in Mendoza there was only one psychoanalyst.

At that time, I had a drive both internal and external, to leave Mendoza, to expand my experiences by continuing my studies in the United States and then to return to Mendoza with a different type of specialization and training. I thought about giving back in some way everything I had learned there, because when I left the faculty, I took an excellent education with me. Besides the unique academic experience of having obtained the assistantship in psychiatry for three or four years, where I learned a lot, I also had my training in psychoanalysis, all the theoretical meetings of Wednesday nights, my supervisions in Mendoza and Buenos Aires, and my presentation of theoretical clinical work at an international congress.

I was quite optimistic when I applied to the Menninger Clinic, a school of psychiatry in the United States. I thought that I would be accepted and go there the following year. To my great surprise, they accepted me two months after applying and having obtained my medical degree, that is, for that same year.

Why did you choose the Menninger?

Etchegoyen had suggested the Menninger and also another school of psychiatry in New York, whose name I don't remember. But as I was interested especially in the issue of social and economic injustices and its impact on anti-social behaviour, the Menninger Clinic was my first choice, especially because of the influence of its great founder, Karl Menninger, famous for his very humanist psychoanalytic culture and with very important texts written on these issues like *Man Against Himself* and later *The Crime of Punishment*, in which he expounds on his understanding without any prejudice about those individuals who commit crimes.

In short, I left Argentina with a very rich psychoanalytic culture and, to my surprise, when I arrived in the United States, I found the level quite mediocre in comparison to what I had left behind. My learning included not only my psychoanalytic training in Mendoza but also all of our practical seminars and lessons with international personalities in the field. With one of my great colleagues Julia Lauzón, who currently lives in Chile, we started group therapy for kids. We realized that parents waited outside, which was a waste, so we decided to simultaneously hold a therapeutic group for parents. At the time, I was not expecting how this would benefit me when I started working in England at the Henderson Hospital, the first therapeutic community created by Maxwell Jones. I had already learned about this in Mendoza.

When I arrived at the Menninger, I had the opportunity to personally meet Maxwell Jones and to review his work. This was part of a series of seminars with scientific personalities from all over the world. As a result, I met for example the great anthropologist, Margaret Mead, who loved to socialize with students. The training was very complete and was also very wisely arranged in the sense that one worked as a psychiatrist for which we were given a stipend, and at the same time, we had the theoretical training which we paid for with the earnings from our clinical work.

But you say it disappointed you.

I had been raised and breast-fed, psychoanalytically speaking, by Melanie Klein, who was not known at all. I think even Jaspers had just been translated into English. There was a very important Latin American group there who were much more sophisticated than the others. The year after I arrived, Otto Kernberg and his wife, Paulina also arrived. I will always remember her for that initial time because although I was doing very well academically, my English was very "primitive", and I had needed to learn it urgently. Paulina was always willing to give me a hand.

In addition, there were totally absurd, personal and professional things happening around me. I was the only female doctor, along with another, also named Estela. Initially we were great friends, but over time all types of conflicts arose that had unconsciously been created by the South American group. Then, I don't remember why, or I don't know what happened, I was the only female doctor who remained among at least sixty male doctors. The women were all nurses or secretaries, but there was no other female doctor. Also, I was young and single, which gave me a few problems because everyone asked me in amazement: "Have you never married?" I, who until then had been so proud of my career, of my independence, had to go through the embarrassment of still being single.

Karl Menninger was very happy with my progress and I shared his passion for social justice. He had written a lot about it and he was very passionate on the subject and knew a lot about it. There are very interesting things that came out of that period, because I arrived in 1962 and stayed there for two years. You must remember that it was the era before the women's liberation movement and the campaigns for civil rights in the United States, so very, very absurd situations arose. When people ask me, what I was doing in the Midwest, almost in the desert, I answer that I am very grateful to have been there, because I think the priorities that apply to life are exactly the same if you are in California, New York or Kansas, maybe, the only difference was in their severity. There were things that happened to me that showed an incredibly high level of prejudice, so much so that I was really disgusted.

When I got to the Menninger, I was assigned as Chief of Service of a mixed patient room and I was put in charge of the staff, who were all black people, except for the matron (head nurse). I must confess that in Argentina I had never seen anyone that was black. Later I found out in a casual way, and not through the reading of the Argentine Constitution as a student in Mendoza, that the immigration of blacks was prohibited. I found out because I had to give a lecture about Argentina and went to the library to look up demographic data for my speech. There I learned that this law existed, similar to the one that existed in Australia. It stated that all immigrants had to be white. Immigrants of a different skin colour were not accepted, a topic I knew nothing about when I left Argentina.

I have always had a vocation for leadership. I do not know if it is innate or acquired, and this has allowed me to get on very well with the people I work with. So, the first thing that occurred to me was to invite all my staff to have lunch at a restaurant close to the hospital. They looked a little amazed and accepted. There was some anxiety that I had glimpses of in the group, but I did not realize the cause of this anxiety. The great mystery was revealed when we got to lunch at a Mexican restaurant where I was welcomed with the words: "You are welcome, but the rest of your group is not". I was speechless, and I was very angry, not only with the restaurant but also with my staff for letting me make such a fool of myself. I was again amazed by the response of my staff, as I found it unexpected. I was told: "But we thought that you being a doctor meant you knew better than anyone else." These racial prejudices extended to the point that I was not allowed to enter with them in places for blacks. They were not allowed to buy property next to the properties of white people. They could however buy big cars and the sales showroom was the only public space that blacks and whites could share. That was democracy.

I managed to rent a very small apartment in a fairly mixed area. There were many Japanese citizens; it was not the time of Japanese prosperity as yet. The owner of my apartment was very proud to have not only a doctor, but one who was in training at the Menninger. This was a most important thing, because very famous actors in Hollywood would come to Topeka to do environmental therapy and the like. Following this disastrous experience at the Mexican restaurant, I began to organize, in my small apartment, a few theoretical seminars for my staff on Wednesday nights. This had been the traditionally allotted night since the time of Freud and also in Mendoza with Etchegoyen. I invited them for a meal and while we ate, we talked about the things that happened during the week. This gave us a space to talk about our patients and their emotional developments. To my dismay, two months later the owner of the apartment came to tell me that there had been complaints from my neighbours about the parties I was holding at my house. "I have never had a party, I don't know where this complaint is coming from" I told him, expressing my confusion, to which he replied: "there are parties here every Wednesday night." Still confused, I told him that they were work meetings, that there was no music or anything that could disturb other neighbours. Then he offered me an alternative that I thought was the most abominable proposition he could make: that all the people who came, all the staff, must enter through the backside of my house. I replied by telling him that he could stuff his apartment into his backside, and I immediately went in search of a new apartment.

In November 1963, when President Kennedy was assassinated, there were again very unexpected situations that arose. The news arrived at noon to our sector, when we were all gathered for lunch, and I don't need to say, it caused a huge commotion. There were unbelievable responses from some staff members. For example, a colleague from South Carolina was visibly excited and even happy that it had happened. It was a very unexpected reaction for the rest of the staff, I do not think anyone had known what was happening in a small town like this one. It was a Friday, and Topeka was not only a small place, but totally flat from every point of view. There were no theaters or cinemas. Once a month a movie was shown for the medical staff in a coliseum that was transformed into a movie theater. I remember perfectly, that on that Friday there was going to be a showing of *A Taste of Honey,* an English movie that we had really been looking forward to. However, it occurred to me that a movie shouldn't be shown just after the announcement of the death of the president. I was used to the fact that when this sort of thing happened in my country, we had to observe total mourning and that other activities like this one were irreverent. So, I met up with a Cuban colleague and we went directly to the coliseum where the film was going to be shown, to tell them that it had been decided that the showing should be cancelled as a sign of respect and mourning. Some of our colleagues did not agree with the decision and they got very angry. The next day, like every Saturday, we had "Dr. Karl's Symposium," which was an open activity where any topic was discussed. It was positive because it allowed us to exchange ideas among ourselves on political and social issues. But that day, the truth was we had no idea of what could happen. Dr. Karl began by saying that he was very proud that the students had decided to cancel the film as a sign of respect for the president's death and that he knew the sacrifice it had meant to us. Then I, who had previously been filled with trepidation about my colleagues and authority figures, felt very relieved.

Despite this sort of occurrence, the truth is that I was not happy, and I felt very badly. I remember that I argued quite a lot with the Argentinian group and at one point I went to see Otto Kernberg and I explained the whole situation to him. He told me something very wise: "Look Estela, make a list of all in favor of staying and another of the things against staying." The longest list was that of things against, and that is how I took the decision to leave the Menninger. However, what I told Dr. Karl was that I wanted to go to London to see if I could do group therapy for a while, or to do the psychotherapeutic training in the Tavistock and then return to the Menninger, even though I did not actually intend to do so. He was very attentive, very understanding, and gave me a letter for Anna Freud, a letter in which, to my surprise, he also told her that when he returned to England they could go horseback riding again together.

Why did you choose England?

England was the "Mecca" for Argentines: The School of Melanie Klein and Bion were absolutely essential, the Tavistock was also a great guiding light, as it had a very special magnetism. When I informed Etchegoyen about my plans, he was not very happy with my decision. He advised me to finish my psychiatric training at the Menninger and then go to London, but I knew it was really a matter of survival.

You were fed up.

I was completely fed up. It was more than boredom, it was like I was in a gap, maybe because I was the only woman who was in training. In addition, there was a competition among the students like I had never seen before, and a great lack of scope for anything else. People spoke about what they wanted to have in three or four years, and everyone said the same thing: a color television, a particular brand of car, a house that was a certain way, and sometimes even a yacht. This was the sort of thing that made me despair. It was a totally "flat" life in cultural terms. I really believed that I was going to suffocate and that I was going to die there. The Argentines had their own group, but they had also 'flattened' themselves. So, I made my decision. I think I had $200 saved up, but I imagined I was going to find work right away. I don't know why, but I had the idea, a totally erroneous one, that if I was accepted by the Tavistock, I was going to find work immediately. Nothing was further from reality. The two centers that existed were the Maudsley, that was totally distanced from psychoanalysis, and the Tavistock, set up as a psychodynamic training center.

Did you know anybody there who could help you?

Well, I had Dr. Karl's letter for Anna Freud, but I never used it. It seemed very unethical to visit Anna when I wanted to do Kleinian psychoanalytic training.

At the beginning it was very hard. Although there were positions for psychiatrists in hospitals, these did not interest me. That said, my first contact with London made me feel very good. I remember it was October 4, 1964, a very sunny day, very nice, and it seemed to me that I felt like I had to have been born here. I believe I was never ambivalent in any way about living in London but arriving in the sixties with all the important things that were happening here in art, in music, was wonderful. There were things that were very ancient and traditional, but at the same time very, very new things, that were very vibrant. I had no interest in money. I don't know where it came from, but I was never worried about money in the sixties, unlike what happens these days, now that everything has changed completely. It was a very liberated life and there was no prejudice about money, in stark contrast to what I had left behind in the United States. This seduced me a lot.

There were good positions available in mental hospitals of the classical type, but of course it did not even occur to me that I could survive that way.

First, I was at the Tavistock for training in groups. As for jobs, I was very lucky, I got one in the therapeutic community of Henderson that was about 40 minutes away by train. I had met Maxwell Jones in Topeka. It was a totally democratic therapeutic community. When I got there it seemed wonderful, an unexpected dream. I could never have imagined a place that would work like it did. It was a community of about 100 people, I mean 100 patients, and we were so many staff members. In addition to traditional positions, there were also social therapists, who were in positions created by Maxwell. You could say that we were two employees for each patient, which was really incredible.

How much did this experience influence your thinking?

Despite my great admiration for this workplace, I never imagined that I would get to work there. It did not even occur to me to think about it until I got in. It was like an unattainable dream: to work with psychopaths in a therapeutic community! Maxwell had tried to change the name to sociopaths, but there is always the stigma of people that act against the law to be, in a certain sense, seen and experimentally recognized. The disordered world of perversion or of the antisocial. In reality it must be understood in an entirely different way from the ethics of our daily lives and understood as the furthest from neurotic people. When Winnicott says that those who commit anti-social acts have a kind of hope in society, what this means is that when they were children, they never felt that their basic needs were recognized, and now they are recognized for something that they do against society.

This is very interesting. For example, when Kennedy was assassinated, Karl Menninger was writing something about the non-identity of the patient who commits criminal acts or crimes. He saw Lee Harvey Oswald, President Kennedy's assassin, as someone who was lost in the world, someone whom no-one had recognized and who suddenly became the most famous person in the world. That is, he had a thorough understanding, a total understanding, which of course is entirely against the attitude of guilt, of judging, which is what always happens in our society. There is always someone who judges. A judge is meant to judge. It is not the psychiatrist's job to judge, or to have "silly compassion". We are meant to have the type of compassion that leads to trying to understand events that are not immediately comprehensible. We are often blinded by the passion of wanting to do something against these people. This is because we automatically identify with the victim and we are predisposed to apply the law of Talion: an eye for an eye and a tooth for a tooth.

But, look, it's as if you understood Menninger, not in Topeka, but at the Henderson. It's funny that you refer to Menninger when you talk about Henderson.

It is the ideology of being able to understand and not to judge. Henderson was a society that was so democratic that there was a clause stating that patients could only stay a year, or two at the maximum, to avoid the possible consequence of being "institutionalized", it was a back-to-front institution.

The day began at 7:45 in the morning with a committee that was chaired by a patient who, by fully democratic vote, had been elected for a month, as the maximum period so that there would be no abuse of power or corruption. That is to say that it was like a transitory institution. The assembly decided by vote and the director of the hospital had the same power as any newly admitted patient. At that first morning session everyone could talk, but with a time limit, there were three minutes dedicated to the doctors, which was the only time we were allowed to talk.

Do you think this fulfilled a therapeutic function?

Of course, because you could see that the patients were taken very seriously into account. They were given so much authority that they necessarily identified with authority. They then could not be against the authority since they themselves were the authority: they were in charge of admission and also of discharge. There were times when I was very angry that some patients were discharged who I thought could have been helped more, but they were discharged because they had broken some rule. These regulations had to be carried out in a very strict, almost religious manner. For example, you could not take an aspirin, you could not smoke in certain places. Each of these things was the result of wisdom born from experience. For example, the "non-smoking rule" was because of a history of arsonists, there had been an occasion when they had tried to set the hospital on fire. The "no aspirin" had to do with the possibly of it leading to the use of any medication or drug that was totally against treatment. Asking a person to keep a secret was another thing that was strictly prohibited, because this could lead to a lack of trust in the system. Everything was done via groups and we all participated in the political and social life of the community. We the doctors also had to be part of the work groups. These groups were in charge of everything, from the cleaning of the clinic, —which was at times a real bother because there were things that were quite dirty— to things like participating in the clinic activities, we all had our participation quota.

The truth is that for me this experience was very different from a Bionian group. Of course, sometimes this led me into great conflicts because I was very influenced by the interpretation of negative transference which for me continues to have a basic and indispensable value, especially with this type of patient. For example, when I arrived, the Medical Director was a man close to retirement age, who was on vacation. When he returned and announced that he was retiring, the totally irrational fantasy of the community was that I had come to replace him, although I was much younger than he was and was also still in training. This generated much indignation in the community, and it made my life very complicated. In my therapy group, the patients went on strike against me. They marched around me and did not allow me to do any interpretation. It was rather dramatic.

Very much a challenge.

Very much a challenge in which, sometimes, quite funny things would turn up. I remember that at one point I was offered the opportunity to travel to Argentina, not only for free but hired as a ship's doctor. I wanted to go to see my father who was not well. The biggest inconvenience to going back was that it was going to take about two months, seven or eight weeks. When I asked for permission at the staff meeting, I was denied because holidays for the personnel were two or three weeks maximum. I concealed my immense frustration and, without saying anything to my colleagues, it occurred to me that I should present a special request to the whole community at a mornings' general meeting. I told them very briefly that I had the opportunity to go see my father, whom I had not seen for some time and who was in poor health, but the problem was that I had to leave for much longer than I was allowed to. To the surprise of the personnel and my colleagues, the patients said to me: "Of course, Estela, you have to go see your father." And that is how, by going over the heads of my colleagues, I could travel to Argentina.

How long did you stay at the Henderson?

I stayed for two and a half years. It was a very rich and difficult experience because at one point we were left without a director of the hospital. There were two or three consultants who were so against authority that the administration of the region that was in charge of the hospital, was never going to give the go-ahead so that one of them could replace him. A kind of very anarchic community was formed for a time. Sometimes very challenging situations presented themselves, but they too were very rich experiences, and we learned a lot from them. Further down the line, Stewart Whiteley arrived. He was a very seasoned and knowledgeable psychiatrist, but also very conventional, so he questioned accepting the position. I think he was not very interested in being in charge of 100 delinquent patients, with all the problems that this entailed. I confronted him and said: "You can be a good psychiatrist anywhere, but if you come here you will find a situation so new and incredibly powerful that you will be able to write, do extremely important things, and this will give you a way into the international world of psychiatry. He still remembers my advice with great esteem. He accepted the job, but in exchange he asked me to stay on longer. In England one must broaden one's horizons. I could have stayed on until I was director of the hospital, but obviously that situation was not going to be happening because I needed another specialization. I had already been interviewed by Hanna Segal, so she could advise me on who could be my analyst, and eventually, continue my training in London. I started analysis five times a week with Leslie Sohn, who was considered a most brilliant psychoanalyst. This was a huge sacrifice because every morning I had to go from Victoria train station, to Sutton in the south, where the Henderson was. I would get back between 5:00 and 6:00 in the afternoon and then go on to my analytic session in the north of London, only to return later to my house in Victoria. They were years of so much sacrifice because I started analysis soon after I arrived to London.

Leslie Sohn was your second analyst.

Yes, he was my second analyst and luckily, I had previously had my first analysis, if not I would have been completely confused about what psychoanalysis was. In my sessions with him, we replicated the situations with my father exactly, that is, both of us shouted at each other. He yelled at me and I yelled at him.

What about?

I've always been very rebellious and independent, right? So, if I challenged any interpretation, as had been my habit in my first analysis, Sohn became very angry. He shouted at me asking how I could contradict him, and I responded in kind to the shouting. A kind of domestic violence was established in his consultation office. That had never happened to me before. I think I formed a maternal relationship with Etchegoyen, whom

I felt gave me so much support, who treated me well in all sorts of very difficult situations. In addition, he never stopped using negative transference. Negative transference was crucial for me.

What a contrast you describe!

Sohn had a very aggressive style. He used to say bizarre things to me, like when he made fun of my clinical experiences at the Henderson.

He disparaged your beliefs.

He disparaged things that I, in my view, saw as very respectable. When Salomón Resnik, who was the only Argentine psychoanalyst in London at the time, found out that I was going to analyze with Leslie Sohn, he strongly advised me not to. He tried to dissuade me. I was very angry because it seemed like tremendous interference and he still reminds me of it. He tried to save me from being a "victim" of Leslie Sohn. However, I was not a victim, but there were some very unorthodox situations. For example, I was a close friend of Che Guevara's sister, who was staying at my house. The only thing Sohn wanted to know during my sessions was about the life of Che Guevara, he was very curious about many things from the left. Sometimes his behavior was so improper for a psychoanalyst, especially a Kleinian "purist"! Though it is possible that this might have worked with psychotic patients or another type of person who he, more or less, converted into his pets. I've talked to three or four colleagues who consider themselves his victims —I cannot mention names, of course—, who were not accepted into the British Institute to do training because he, despite being their psychoanalyst, had been against it, although they could have become excellent psychoanalysts.

I believe it was fated, in quite an interesting sense in analytical terms, that I had not been able to train as a psychoanalyst of the International Psychoanalytical Association (IPA). For example, shortly after I left Mendoza, our group was granted the category of center of psychoanalytic training so all my colleagues at that time became psychoanalysts. Another unsuccessful attempt was when I talked to Mimi Langer before I left for Topeka, to see if I could continue my psychoanalytic training with her on my return. She agreed, but when I wrote to confirm the possibility of it happening, I received a letter from her that said she was very sorry, she had assumed that I was leaving for good and no longer had space for me. Despite me never being warned or advised to not try out for the British Institute, or that I should try later, it was obvious that Sohn was against accepting me.

How long were you with Sohn, and why did you stay?

I was in analysis with him for about 4 or 5 years, I don't remember. I'm sure it was until 1969, because I was in analysis five times a week when I met my husband. Finally, I left suddenly, and that is how I ended my analysis with him.

But you suffered constantly.

I imagine that something must have happened from the beginning. I was very much against group therapy work. I did not agree with the therapeutic community or with the training in Tavistock. I had started doing group work with Bob Gosling and all his comments during the sessions, that could not be considered interpretations, were very negative, except for the fact, really very Kleinian, which did not allow other activities.

He was a Kleinian purist.

A total purist. He started shouting at me like my father did when I was young, when I was a teenager, so it was a repetition of that. When I met my husband, he was also in analysis but with a Freudian. Of course, this was fiercely denigrated by Sohn. I went on to apply to the institute many times, but they did not accept me.

What was the first time like? Who interviewed you?

The first time was Wilfred Bion, who ended the interview in twenty minutes. I told him something about groups and I was so fascinated with the group work that he ended the interview then, saying that in that case it was better that I continue with it. I don't even remember who the others were that interviewed me the other times, but then the letters arrived saying they had not accepted me as a candidate.

How did you understand that they had not accepted you?

I don't know, I don't really understand it.

How did you feel at that moment?

Well, I felt really badly. From the beginning of my career I told myself that I was going to be a very good psychoanalyst and that I had all the conditions to be one. Adam Limentani, who was one of my supervisors at the Portman, was very determined with the idea that I had to have my psychoanalytic training, so he pushed me enthusiastically to apply again, and for that purpose he sent me to see Pearl King, who became my third analyst. The truth is that I did not find in her the professional fervor of Horacio Etchegoyen either, I think I was appreciated by her and she saw me more as a colleague.

You didn't feel like she was an analyst?

I did not feel like she was an analyst, I felt she gave me a lot of support, there was even a kind of human affection that I also felt, but I do not think it was like the psychoanalytic experience I had had before. When they decided to not accept me to the Institute for the third time, Adam Limentani and Pearl King, were at a psychoanalytic meeting in Paris. In other words, fate intervened again. If they had been at the meeting where they decided who got in, they would have accepted me. Of course, I felt very badly, I felt rejected, I felt very depressed. I felt this although at the same time, my personal life was going well. After a period of getting to know each other and working together, my future husband and I decided to get married and had a son.

Very sadly and unexpectedly, my husband died when Daniel, our son, was 9 months old. I was in a very critical situation on many and diverse levels: I had no money, I had no home of my own, and I had no job, because when we got married we had decided to have a big family. I immediately decided to investigate the possibilities of getting a position and with this intention I went to see Dr. Gosling, who was in charge of the Tavistock. Gosling told me there was a vacancy at the Portman Clinic and that's how I started working there in 1971. Influenced by Limentani, who was in charge of the clinic at the time and was my supervisor, I went to see Pearl King, I think two or three years later when my son was three years old. I remember that it was a great support for me, but I was not impacted by her. She respected my mourning, but I don't really understand well why it did not leave any mark on me.

What I have to acknowledge though, is that it is possible that they might have been on the right track. Now, I cannot see myself in an orthodox psychoanalytic practice. I do not know if I could have written *Mother, Madonna, Whore* if I had to adhere to psychoanalytic tenets. But the truth is that I had a very, very bad time. However, I have reached a level of independence that has been much more convenient for my area of work. It took me many years to become aware that it is possible that they gave me the opportunity to think more independently.

You mentioned Limentani as someone who supported you, who pushed you to continue your psychoanalysis, this time with Pearl King.

I think that for him, it would have been a great source of pride if I became a psychoanalyst and that it was, more than anything, his enthusiastic support, than my own motivations, that led me to apply again. I don't know, I don't really understand why I was not accepted, when so many other people, some quite mediocre, were accepted. But I think it is possible that, after all is said and done, consciously or unconsciously, my professional life has had a more fruitful development by not being part of a society that expects a type of submission that I did not want. I did not want to submit.

It's as if in some way the institution did not have the digestive system necessary to be able to assimilate you, right? Because, as you have said so well, certain very mediocre people were afraid that you defied the canons. But anyway, I ask myself what the meaning of this is. However, Limentani was also president of the IPA, I think it was a risk for him to propose your name, right?

Of course, Limentani was president of the IPA and had great influence. By chance or whatever, he was not in London at the crucial moment when it was decided whether I would be accepted or not. I do not know what the outcome would have been, but when I published *Mother, Madonna, Whore*, I was invited to a scientific meeting to discuss it with psychoanalyst colleagues. Also, as you know, I have been invited by many psychoanalytic organizations, for example, by the IPA Committee on Women and Psychoanalysis (COWAP), which is a direct strand of the IPA. This is to say, that despite not having done psychoanalytic training, I have known how to earn professional respect. Besides, it is very interesting that with the British Association of Psychotherapists (BAP) the possibility has opened for a few psychotherapists to become direct members of the IPA.

The BAP is now a component society of the IPA.

I do not know for sure because due to illnesses that I had over the same time period when one could apply, I was unable to. So, once again fate, so to speak, intervened to impede a possibility to enter the IPA.

You have had three very different analyses. A first analysis with Horacio Etchegoyen, who became the president of the IPA; a second analysis with Leslie Sohn, a prominent Kleinian; and then after that with Pearl King, who was secretary of the IPA and one of the leading figures in British psychoanalysis. How do you compare these three analytical experiences?

If I consider the strictly professional, the character of Horacio Etchegoyen stands out, his analysis as well, but it was very hard. It was very, very hard for me. It was an analysis in which I was subjected daily to all kinds of interpretations that generated a lot of rebellion in me. However, as this was a very knowledgeable man, I felt good about it. Leslie Sohn had a great reputation, but our combination was a really explosive mix. At times I could not believe it, it was fully-fledged fighting, plus I felt humiliated. I have already told you about his curiosity around political issues and that I had Che Guevara's sister in my house. When I met the film director Tony Richardson, who wanted to make a film about Che, Sohn wanted to know more and more about it, which made me feel like this man was more interested in those things than in my analysis, as if he wanted to get involved in my life. In addition, there were very funny things that happened, for example, once we met in the theatre and he did not recognize me. I don't understand exactly what happened, I don't know. That said, there are also people who have been in analysis with Leslie Sohn and it has gone very well, both men and women.

I wonder why you stayed with him for so much time.

I think I was hoping that it would be a sort of guarantee to then be able to enter the Institute. I also think that I was afraid to leave, I don't remember, it's as if I have erased everything, because I erase bad experiences. I had known him socially before and I thought that could been an obstacle. When I went I asked him if he could take me, he said yes, that he did not mind at all.

And you have told me that Pearl King was a very good person, but she did not do analytic work with you.

Exactly, but I think it's possible that it was that way due to the circumstances I was going through at the time. I had become a widow and my son was about two or three years old when I went to see her, it is possible that she felt in some way maternal, and that there was no other way, I don't know.

We met at the Portman clinic. I was the Senior Registrar when you started to work there.

Do you remember that when I got the job of medical assistant, you were the first one I supervised? I had as many responsibilities in that position as if I was a consultant but it was poorly paid. It was a fixed position, but there was no way to be promoted and move up the ladder. After being a medical assistant for a long time, a consultant, called Dr. Edwards, died. I applied for his job, with the support of all my colleagues. I had already completed my entry requirements to the Royal College of Psychiatrists, for which I had had to do all the revalidation exams and I did them, despite all the difficult situations in my life. Imagine, I was told clearly by the administration that I could lose my job security. I was told, "you realize that if you are in the running for this new position, you will lose that of medical assistant and if you are not accepted you will be out on the street". I told them, "Yes", but also that I believed I could work as a consultant since my qualifications allowed me to do so. Of course, this was before the time of political correctness. These days they could not have allowed themselves to make this type of comment.

I do not know how to rate that experience, because it was really horrible. Besides being the only woman who applied, I was the only one born in a different country. I don't want to say "foreigner" because I do not like to feel foreign here and I have never been made to feel like that in any other jobs I've had in London. Six or seven men applied with me, some very well-known. For example, one of them was in charge of the Marlboro

Clinic. We were all in a room full of cigarette smoke, having coffee with awful milk, waiting to be interviewed. As always, my turn was last because of my last name. Everyone told me about their interviews when they came out afterwards. When I was interviewed, I was asked difficult questions, questions that today are not asked. The first thing that the interviewer asked me was: "Looking at your resume, we can see that you are a widow with a very young child. How can you even think about applying for a position with such responsibility?" And I looked at him and said precisely this: "I am already working with this type of responsibility, but poorly paid. I know I have more than enough training to be a consultant and I also need a job where they can pay me more because I have my son, who is totally dependent on me, as you said, so I cannot afford the luxury of not working".

At that moment he realized that he had made me very angry, so he began to explain to me that his wife had had many problems in her personal life because she had neglected her children a little for her career. He began to tell me about his personal life in front of the entire panel! After, I learned from Ismond Rosen, who had been my supervisor, that he had told him: "Professor, do you realize the talent that Dr. Welldon has? You have just told her all about your private life. The advantage that she has is that everyone tells her their private thoughts and patients, even the most difficult ones, reveal all their problems." When the interview ended, I did not know if I had got the job or not, but I went to ask the other men who were being interviewed if they had to answer questions about their personal lives, for example, how many children they had, or what they do in their homes. No one had been asked those questions, so I felt very hurt for having been subjected to such a prejudiced interrogation.

Happily, times have changed. You say Ismond Rosen gave you great support in that interview.

He told me that he was very happy to have been able to support me because we had similar professional interests. He had written a book about group therapy and also on perversions.

Mervin Glasser also supported you, but your relationship with him afterwards was not easy.

It was a very difficult relationship, even though we respected each other a lot. He was considered the best of all, but we had many problems. I think that I had a much more open view of therapy, while for him it seemed a kind of ivory castle, which no one could approach. This became more visible when I started with the European symposium, after having met several colleagues interested in the subject at a conference in Oxford in 1979.

How do you elaborate your ideas?

Well, I have always elaborated my ideas based on my clinical work. I keep records of everything I hear, what I see in patients, in my interaction with them. My ideas are based on rigorous clinical work. This is very important for psychoanalytic theory, which is a very valuable tool to deepen my understanding of the kind of cases that have always interested me, those of patients with social disorders. I think that psychoanalysis is the only tool for understanding these patients. There is no other theory, there is no other type of work that can be done. That is why the concept of guilt is very important. Many people said that these people should be sorry for what they did, that they have no sense of guilt, but from a psychoanalytic perspective one can understand that there are ways of acting-out that are very self-destructive, though from the outside, superficially, they do not seem to be. This is something that people tend to forget or ignore.

There are three areas in which I have focused my work. One of these is based on the understanding of perversion, which has resulted in a totally new concept, that of female perversion. This came out of my work in an out-patient clinic that treats patients with antisocial and violent problems. The Portman Clinic treats patients who commit acts against the law. Most of them are men who had a very precarious relationship with their mothers. Very often they were subjected to some form of neglect, physical and sexual abuse, abandonment, and overprotection.

We are used to listening to young girls that with total candor say, and repeat with great fervor, that they want to have a child in order to have someone who loves them. That is to say, in their minds and fantasies, the baby is a kind of fetish that is at the mercy of caprice, of the inconsistent need of a mother who is waiting for a child to love her unconditionally. Unfortunately, things do not happen this way. The child is born, and as we know, this new being has its own needs and demands that are totally unexpected for these women who so longed to have them, without thinking about what they should give and sometimes sacrifice to become mothers. We know that one of the most important parental or maternal "normalizing" functions is to help and stimulate the processes of individuation and independence. But in these cases, the exact opposite occurs. That is, for these children it is impossible to create a sense of identity. They have a false self. It is as if they cannot allow themselves to have their own identity. This led me to think a lot about what was going on that could not be registered or, even more, that could not be recognized or conceptualized, this kind of harmful motherhood. What happens to these women when they become mothers?

Now, despite being closely interrelated, you need to realize that pregnancy and becoming a mother are two different things. There are women who have an internal need to have the experience of being pregnant, because this will provide them with concrete evidence that the inner part of themselves is not damaged, not destroyed, just the opposite, it is absolutely perfect. But when the child is born, these mothers want to give the child up for adoption or leave it. This is why newborns are frequently found left in public places. I do not think we should talk about these women as demonic or bad, because they themselves have felt very unappreciated. They have not felt valued for being women. This is why I always say that to achieve a full understanding of this type of motherhood, we must go back at least three generations.

Another way of wanting to be a mother may be to conform to a desire for absolute control of the child. When faced with this, the child wants to rebel, though sometimes he or she cannot. This is observed very acutely in the transference: they always have to be in control of the situation, they tell you when the session begins and ends, they maneuver in all sorts of ways, consciously and unconsciously, so as not to fall back on or repeat the situation of trusting someone, especially someone in charge of authority.

I believe that the origin of perversions has to do with a very primitive depression that goes back to birth: these people have never felt loved or welcomed. Then they have the unhealthy desire to leave a mark, to do something that identifies them, to have an identity, even if it is an identity that is not a good one, it is important that it looks dangerous and very risky.

It is well-known that as soon as we are confronted with perverse actions that appear in the newspapers, there is a totally automatic response: to judge, never to understand. I want to make it clear that we are talking about perversion as a psychoanalytic, psychodynamic concept, and not as something moral, that is, we have to use understanding, comprehension, in our clinical work. For example, my prior observation that perversion is rooted in the attempt to escape from very deep depression is easy to understand when we observe that the acting out, the perversion or the criminal act has a manic result that is used as a weapon against depression. In this sense, it is a manic defense. Another example is that there are many forms of prostitution, both male and female, but there is one form of prostitution in which the woman feels very depressed without knowing it and she has to go out and get someone who wants her body, without caring at all about anything else. This situation gives her a feeling of wellbeing that is as short as it is false. I say that it is false because it disappears very quickly, and it becomes a new feeling of depression, of disgust with herself, which leads to a vicious cycle that occurs in her inner mind.

There is a characteristic of perversions that consists of taking risks. Here we are talking about people who occupy high-ranking public positions that go from fame to shame. It is the case of the public official who suddenly finds himself discovered in acts and situations in which he has broken social conventions. Another example of this are the pedophile Catholic priests. The scandal has to do with not expecting it from these people. What happens is that these positions can hold a great attraction for people who have these psychopathological disorders.

What is forensic psychotherapy?

Forensic psychotherapy is the bridge or association that is established between psychoanalytic theory and legal medicine. Its purpose is to understand through psychoanalytic concepts what happens in the internal world of patients with antisocial behaviors, that break and transgress the law in a particular way and position themselves against society in general. Instead of punishing, the purpose of forensic psychotherapy is to understand, although this does not mean to forgive or to sanction what has been done. The acknowledgement that these individuals have an internal world is essential and the driving force is to reach a deep understanding of what the origin of these antisocial behaviors is. This means that one must change from a judgment perspective to one of understanding.

This was the most important goal of the Portman Clinic since its inception in 1933. But there wasn't an academic or professional institution specialized on forensic psychotherapy. When I went to a conference in Oxford on Law and Psychiatry in 1979 or 1980, I learned that patients had more confidence in their lawyer than in their psychiatrist. They felt safer with their lawyer since their psychiatrist could subject them to treatment with electroshock. I was very lucky to meet and talk with other professionals from the continent who worked in this field and who also had a psychoanalytic perspective. It was then that the idea of an annual meeting in the Portman Clinic started, the European Symposium, which was held ten times over the following ten years, after which I founded, along with other European colleagues, the International Association for Forensic Psychotherapy. This idea of internationalization was born because it seemed easier and more viable to create an international institution than a national one, which is a bit ridiculous, but that is how it was. I put the motion forward at the Belgian congress, supported by a group of colleagues, who were very loyal to the cause. We have now completed twenty years of uninterrupted work, which we celebrated with the organization of a congress on the theme "Murder in Mind" in Edinburgh.

This association was organized long ago by former students of a course that I founded at the Portman Clinic, supported by the former director of the British Postgraduate Medical Federation, Professor Sir Michael Peckham. I had told him I had the idea of creating a course for professionals working in the forensic field with all kinds of criminals. It would be a wide range of professionals from therapists of art, drama, music, nurses, psychologists, psychiatrists, prison employees and employees of mental hospitals, and any other institutions that deal with these disorders, and use psychoanalytic understanding instead of a punitive vision.

I had many difficulties with creating this course. There were two aspects: On the one side, were those who came from forensic medicine who thought that it would not work because integration was absolutely absurd. On the other side, there were those who came from psychoanalysis, who thought more or less the same but based on a totally purist conceptualization of psychoanalysis. They thought that this effort of psychoanalytic comprehension could be seen as modified psychoanalysis or used too pragmatically. Suddenly all of this changed when I was invited by Sir Michel Peckham to present my innovative ideas. This course was created thanks to him, this professor of Oncology, who is also a painter, who saw this as a creative mix. It seemed incredible to him that this had not been done before. The first time I saw him he had a 15-minute meeting blocked off for me. It turned into three hours of very intense work. I left there not only with the structure of the course but also with a list of other organizations that would support it. He was a very active professional, who did not delay with things, so we were able to put this course together very quickly, despite frequent disagreements with many colleagues at the clinic. At first there were all kinds of internal problems, of protocol and so on, but as there were so many people involved, and very important people, we could put it all together in a very short time. We had to overcome quite a bit of resistance. I had many fights with Mervin Glasser and with other colleagues who, based on a purist conception of psychoanalysis, thought that we were going to contaminate it. From this arose the condition that people coming to the course had to be in psychoanalytic psychotherapy. Professionals of all kinds came from all over. In short, a gap that had really existed was filled.

After a while, Peckham was named professor at the London University College. Obviously, the course was also offered at this university, but the demands multiplied very intensively and extensively. We had to fill out a long list of forms and other things, which took us a lot of time and effort, but we got it all done. It was very impressive to belong to the London University College, a very important university, also with many resources, and we were very proud that the course was to become a university course with all the necessary academic requirements. I call this time the golden decade, because I had ten years of teaching with fantastic students. Former students from this course have written many books and are now university professors. They have become university professors who are bastions of the International Association for Forensic Psychotherapy.

Unfortunately, this course has ceased to exist. A year before I retired, I left a colleague in charge of the course, so it could continue as it was, but over time everything changed. He was relieved of his position at the University College, they eliminated the university structure that had given him a lot of academic flight, and they got rid of all the teachers and other external professionals who were great stalwarts of the course. This was not done diplomatically. Now the course is not taught at all due to a lack of interested students, even though I have evidence to the contrary. Even now a lot of people call me asking where they can do this kind of training and they complain that it does not exist.

Was there a leadership problem?

I think that the people at the clinic did not believe in this project, which was the same problem as before. They felt more important and wondered why they had to be under the rules of another institution. They calculated that students were interested in the clinic but not in the university. I do not know if that was true, it is very easy to seduce students to say something like that. Now, thanks to former students, a branch at the Royal College of Psychiatrists has been created that has begun to develop a series of cultural events, including events on forensic aspects in film and the opera.

You say there was a mixture of arrogance and provincialism.

Definitely. An incredible arrogance that also exists in the psychoanalytic institution, I believe that psychoanalysts are very arrogant, but now they are going through a crisis. What is happening in many parts of Europe is that the number of sessions of analysis has been reduced from five to three times a week. This is an indication that psychoanalysis as it is, cannot work for much longer.

You said that Glasser did not agree with the course.

Glasser did not agree at all that it be made so accessible to "the masses", that was the idea. There is a very deep problem of hierarchy.

You are speaking of purist arrogance, of the idea of being an aristocracy.

Yes, but now things have changed. Now visiting days are organized during which even drinks are offered to sell you psychoanalysis. It's a pity about what is happening.

Tell me more about the British Association of Psychotherapists (BAP).

There were people who said they were going to train themselves as psychotherapists because they were interested in being completely free from psychoanalytic rigor, in having sessions twice and not five times a week. Now that the possibility of becoming a psychoanalyst has opened up, many of those who had said they would never enter a psychoanalytic institution have accepted and become psychoanalysts. This shows that they felt handicapped. For example, the BAP clinical seminars could be taught by the graduates of the same institution, but the theoretical seminars always had to be taught by psychoanalysts.

What about feminism?

The truth is that in this we also find paradoxes. When my book *Mother, Madonna, Whore* was published in 1988, there was a feminist bookstore in London that refused to sell it because they immediately assumed that I was demonizing women by writing something that questioned the veracity of the maternal instinct and exposing for the first time authentic stories of some women who in a state of despair beat their children and even sexually abused them, as they felt powerless in the face of the needs of their children. Only when they read the book well did they realize that my intention was to expose a very serious problem that had been totally ignored.

In general, I think that women have been fighting for many things for a long time. There are things that have been fixed but there are others in which no significant changes can be observed. Sometimes we do not appreciate our achievements, or we take them for granted. Female competition can also be very cruel and, as usual, the improvements have been achieved in the highest social classes. There is still a lot that can be done in the lower social classes.

I think the most important thing is the equal pay between men and women. This has led to all sorts of problems too, because now women expect to finish a career to have children later, so they are able to have a more independent life. In contemporary marriages, people are much more prepared to share everything. But women are often unequally responsible. For this reason, we have to inculcate the idea of sharing all the domestic chores in boy children.

It is very important to give women the option of being mothers, or not. The problem is that we are subjected to very significant cyclical changes like menopause, which appear very threatening in women who were convinced of their desire to not have children and who suddenly find themselves without the biological possibility anymore. This produces a very deep kind of ambivalence with a consequent state of frustration and unhappiness.

It has been over twenty years since your book Mother, Madonna, Whore, came out. How have things changed since then?

As regards the pathology of women, maternity, and those sorts of things, I think they have changed a lot. In 1988 these issues were not recognized, much less defined. The problem existed, but was not visible. As I said before, there is an immediate and tacit identification with the unloved child and a rejection of the woman, who knows from the beginning that she will not be listened to and then who completely isolates herself. The fact that she is unable to talk about it makes the problem get worse.

Now they are being listened to much more, many more cases like these have come to light. Something very encouraging and rewarding has been happening recently. I listened to a program called "Woman's Hour" on the BBC, Radio 4. A family doctor spoke of the change that there has been in relation to the way postpartum depression is understood. It has always been taken for granted that it was due to hormonal issues, but now the pregnant woman is asked how she feels about pregnancy. That is to say, it is not taken for granted that pregnancy is always a welcome thing. Now we recognize that women can be, consciously or unconsciously, uncomfortable with pregnancy.

It is assumed as something natural that there is nothing more wonderful for a woman than to get pregnant.

This is a myth that began a long time ago. It is associated with the image of the Madonna who became pregnant through the work of the Holy Spirit, who became a mother without sex, that is the whole imprint of religion. Female sexuality is eradicated when the woman becomes a mother.

Maternity makes sex disappear?

Yes, it makes sex disappear in the minds of others, it is a continuation of the myth of the Madonna. Can you see it?

Maternity makes all women virgins.

In the opinion of other people, yes, but I think that the problem is much more complex, because in my latest research I have confirmed the fact that the pregnant body makes others very envious, both men and women. Envy is not the only result, but also acts of perversion and sadism. The pregnant woman has more problems of domestic violence, of family violence. It's very interesting because there is a lot of talk about sexuality, but talking about mature, conscious, heterosexual sexuality, that leads to pregnancy, is avoided. Why is it so hard to imagine that a woman can do horrible things to her children when ultimately the husband can mistreat her, can humiliate her, and at the end of it all she should stay home with their children who are the weakest? Subsequently the women find release for their rage with the children, the most vulnerable, through identification with the aggressor. I think it's not very difficult to figure this out. Why is it so difficult to accept it? I think it's because of our idealization of the mother, because we all want to become totally perfect mothers and that does not exist.

I was wondering about these new forms of maternity. Nowadays technology seems to have really drawn nearer to religion as it is possible that a virgin gets pregnant.

I do not know. It is possible that sometimes women hold a kind of contempt towards men, a feeling that he is not needed. There are also all these new investigations about pregnancy in men. There are investigations to see if it is possible for male pregnancy to occur in the kidney. This possibility exists. I believe that it is not a man or a woman thing, it is pregnancy that produces envy.

That is to say, when a woman becomes pregnant, women who are around her feel envious.

Also, for example, when women go to collect children at school, those who have not been able to have, or who have decided not to have more children, watch those they see pregnant, with great envy.

Now, you are saying that it is the envy of pregnancy, not of maternity, because if a woman has a little child, that is not as envied as the pregnant woman is. The situation of being pregnant is what produces the envy.

Yes, that's it. It is because of the evidence of fertilization after a sexual encounter that has procreated a new being.

This is the moment when there is most violence.

In which it may appear, when it can spark greater violence, yes.

In couples.

Especially in couples. There are also attacks on pregnant women outside the home, but most are in the home.

In times of war in the former Yugoslavia, soldiers used to stab the pregnant women in their belly with a bayonet as part of the extermination of the 'bad' race. It is an act that terrifies, but at the same time it is frequent. It would be easier to shoot them. What is the particular meaning of stabbing the bayonet in the belly?

There are also very famous cases, for example, that of Charles Manson with Sharon Tate, Roman Polanski's wife. She was obviously pregnant, almost nine months, and they attacked her in the belly. There were other people and they were killed too, but not like that.

It's as if it incites great envy and there is the need to make the thing that makes you envious disappear.

Exactly, you have to destroy it.

The need for control, of a non-criminal control. Did you talk about this in your new book?

Well, my new book has contributions from all of my didactic experiences, it has things from the course that I started in 1981, and also from the International Association of Forensic Psychotherapy. This week we have our 21st congress in Venice. The theme from last year was very interesting, "Murder in Mind". It was a great success even though it was held in Edinburgh on the same day as the Royal Wedding, and it wasn't only the Royal Wedding, it was two consecutive holiday weekends. This year is politically opportune: "Corruption, collusion and deception, attacks on the mind", we will see clinical cases and several examples on the subject of corruption, for example the potential corruption that may exist between the therapist, the patient, and the health system.

I think that when you talk about corruption you immediately think about politics.

Yes, but corruption also occurs with this type of patient and in reality, corruption, collusion, and disappointment exist in all walks of life, in any sphere. Of course, in politics, you see things more clearly, for example with Berlusconi in Italy or the work of the judges against the Mafia. I just finished watching an Argentinian film, *Carancho,* in which corruption is seen around traffic accidents. After an accident occurs, public agents appear and offer to help the wounded to claim their insurance. In this way it easily converted into a criminal system, much less money is given to the injured person, and these agents keep most of the money. You can see everything together in this situation: corruption, collusion, and deception.

In our experience with social security, I imagine that it's the same in the private sector, the type of patient that we have refuses to accept responsibility for the problem that they themselves have caused. They then try to stop the action of justice, with a sort of obscured participation of the therapist, which gives rise to collusion.

Where are you now in terms of your practice?

At the moment I am very active in the preparation of our congresses. My last book has been well received and I have been invited to discuss it in many places. This has given me the opportunity of disseminating what we do. I think it is very important that all the people who work with those patients who have committed crimes or antisocial behavior, have a forum where they can talk to each other, because sometimes this type of patient can make you feel very silly or that you are in the middle of a corrupt situation, that you cannot talk openly. There are all kinds of difficulties that therapists sometimes are ashamed to disclose, because therapists who work with normal people or neurotics do not realize it. I think it is important to have a place and an occasion so that they can talk to each other, especially those who work in jails or hospitals. This is in relation to conferences. On the other hand, I still have my clinical work and the supervision in hospitals and prisons. This allows me to be aware of what is happening in those areas.

Tell me about your last book.

Playing with Dynamite has as subtitle: *A Personal Approach to the Psychoanalytic Understanding of Perversion, Violence and Crime.* I discuss, in great detail in this book, what I consider to be perversions in men and women, which is quite different or is in direct controversy with what other psychoanalytic authors have claimed previously.

My work has always been based on the clinical work, that is, I see and listen to what is happening. I think that it is very important to use psychoanalytic theory, but also that sometimes you have to modify it. Let me explain. Throughout all my research on perversion I've noticed that there are very important concepts that have not been defined very clearly. For example, before they used to talk of a splitting which means a person is generally not conscious of what they are doing. I am talking about an encapsulation because I want to highlight that there is a part of the person that has no relationship with the other parts.

Why do you differentiate between splitting and encapsulation?

Because in the case of splitting it is understood that the person does not know what is happening. I believe it is just the opposite: the left hand knows what the right is doing, what happens is that it is kept encapsulated, like a part that they cannot show anyone but themselves.

I also emphasize the moral aspect a lot, I believe that the moral aspect does not occupy any place in perversions. Many years ago, when I arrived at the Portman Clinic, I had a clinical case that taught a lot to me and my older colleagues. I remember that he was a young man, very attractive, with a completely independent career, and he had been married very recently. We asked ourselves what the reason for the referral was to evaluate him. It turns out that by chance it had been discovered —in general these mysteries are discovered this way—, when he and his wife, newly married, moved to a new house, that he received via post a type of publication that had to do with the corporal use of rubber articles. In the session he had described to me how he had to cover himself completely with rubber, including his face and ears, so there was a total absence of sensorial stimuli, so he could reach the point of ejaculation in the moment in which he was really between life and death. A way to describe this situation occurred to me: "to dance with death", which is different from another analytic author who calls it "flirting with death", because when dancing with death the body is involved in the situation, it is acting with the body, which is another of the important characteristics for perversion to work.

At that time, I was very young, I had no experience with cases of perversion and I was really amazed by the description of the quality and characteristics of the rubber that he used. On Saturday of that week after seeing this patient, I went shopping in Soho as I often did. It is the London area where very rich exotic foods can be found, as well as all types of peculiar things that have to do with sexuality. While there, I felt impelled to enter a shop with sexual items to try to understand more. I was greatly surprised, I found exactly what this man had told me he used. Seeing this rubber article gave me a guide to begin to understand what was happening in his unconscious. Then, with great pride, I went to our clinical presentation at the Portman on the following Friday to talk about what I had done expecting general approval. The opposite happened, I was so ashamed and humiliated that they made me get very angry, because what was interpreted was that I had entered into a perverse collusive transference with the patient, that I had made myself his partner in perversion. Wrapped up in my anger I was greatly inspired and I said: "I will accept that I was transferentially compromised in this type of perversion if you can explain to me the type of rubber that this patient uses exactly. If you can't, then I will assume that in reality my motivation was epistemological and not a perverse and collusive transfer". To my great relief, everyone, all my colleagues, even the most experienced, believed the same as what I had believed of this rubber before seeing it: that its consistency was the same as was used in the making of wetsuits, for underwater activities. On the contrary, in my scientific research I had discovered that this rubber was a very delicate substance, like a second skin that covered the person from head to toe. It allows them to have complete sensory annulment that I immediately associated with the concept of Elizabeth Bick, who spoke about the second skin. This discovery was invaluable in this case, because the man felt that this skin was protecting him, was containing him. It was something that he experienced within himself, a kind of *aphanisis*, as if he were going to disappear. I was saved by a whisker, thank God, because I really felt very humiliated by the kind of interpretation they had done, for which after, of course, I was vindicated.

I remember that one day, talking with this patient about what he saw in his wife in erotic terms, he told me that one time when he was watching television in the living room he had felt a very important and immediate erotic desire, and that he had had to make love to his wife there, in that moment, in that room, on the floor. Well, the truth is that I did not think it was that bad, but he explained that what he'd been watching on television had nothing to do with a romantic scene or anything related. It was the escape artist Houdini, risking his life in a box at Niagara Falls.

It was important then to investigate and understand why he had had this kind of bizarre response to the show, what was happening to him. Since I had only worked in the clinic for a short time, I had a very small consultation room and I felt in the transference and countertransference, an almost uterine sensation, something that was intertwining us both. I felt it so strongly, I asked him how his birth had been. I could see he was deeply shocked by the question and he replied that he thought it had caused many problems, but as his mother was alive, he would ask her. In the next session he explained in great detail that he was born very prematurely, that he had weighed only a kilo and a half, and because of this he had been put in an incubator where he spent six months balancing between life and death. During the time he lost weight and then recovered it. This topic took several months and years of sessions. To explain it briefly, for this person the only way to survive this whole thing was unrepresentable. I'm talking here about Norberto Marucco's idea of repetition of the unrepresentable. The use of the rubber protection was the closest thing to being in the incubator that had been responsible for his survival. The lack of any kind of sensation led to the repetition of the situation of being between life and death. The death instinct, which is questioned by many psychoanalysts, appears with noticeable evidence in perversions. In this type of person, it is very evident that there is a need to position themselves between life and death. In such circumstances, the only ethic is survival, and I ask myself what that has to do with morality.

I remember that at the time there was something dramatic that happened that came out in all the newspapers. It was the case of a member of parliament who had accidentally died of autoerotic asphyxiation. He had been found suffocated by a type of bond and ligature, and also had an apple in his mouth. This led to all kinds of mocking speculations. In this example we see that the origin of a perversion has to do with survival. That is why I think that perversion is not the replacement of a psychosis, it is actually a result of a great depression and a manic intent to avoid death, which is why the same action is repeated again and again forever.

So, I think this compulsive, repetitive action, which does not support any change of surroundings and that is also protected as an encapsulation, because no one else is aware of it, is also seen as a form of mania, it appears to avoid depression resulting from a lack of something. It is not a depression brought on by the disappearance of something that a person had and no longer has, it is a depression brought on by something that they never had, it is a total lack (absence). Sometimes this is represented in art. For example, I saw a retrospective exhibition at the Tate Modern gallery, a work by Juan Muñoz, a deceased Spanish artist, called "El Pasamanos". It is a stair railing that helps one feel protected and which one holds on to, so movement is safe. However, on this handrail there was a knife that could hurt you. This knife is totally paradoxical and sinister, uncanny. I compared it to what happens to a new-born with a mother who is experiencing a very distressing desire to hurt her child. That is, when the person responsible for protecting the child is doing all the opposite, putting him or her in contact with a life and death situation. This artist has been able to convey in a very clear and bizarre way what happens in situations in which a person feels betrayed by the one who they should be able to count on the most.

This is what makes the treatment of perversions so difficult.

Of course, it is very difficult, because these people also have a great talent for making jokes, an indication of mania. So, if therapists are not well trained in relation to this type of pathology, it is very easy for them to be caught up in being empathetic, to laugh at a joke made by the patient and when they laugh to realize that they have laughed at the patient.

I was thinking about the use of perversion itself as a tool of seduction.

Yes, one of its functions is to lead the therapist so he does not see the perverse side, but he does see the manic. We see then that the use of negative transference is very important. It is not possible to treat it unless you have the courage to work with negative transference. If not, the patient will lose any kind of confidence that he or she may have had, and it will again be a bitter triumph for him or her, which will succeed in hiding the depression.

We must also be very careful with containment of their anxieties, because it may be that this anxiety that has to do with depression, will eventually be represented in suicide. This must be taken into account always. Interpretation of negative transference has to be accompanied simultaneously by something positive that one sees in the patient. It has to be seen from both angles, the patient has to see himself "with warts and all". He has to see all the bad things as well as the good he has. I believe that the negative therapeutic reaction, which Horacio Etchegoyen speaks of and which shows itself in this type of patient, is very important. The truth is that sometimes those of us who have had experience with this type of patient, realize that when we thought we could not do anything more, is when the patient begins to react positively and encourages the type of therapy that he or she needs. This can last for many years, but the interpretation of the negative always has to be done. If the person does not feel that this can be done, then it is impossible.

And how do you see the therapeutic possibilities?

Well, one thing that actually continues to work very well is mixed group therapy. If you have two people who have been involved in fraud, they will recognize themselves in each other because they have things in common that they share. They will then take interpretations from one another as they see themselves as a kind of mirror. They can make interpretations about things that the psychotherapist has probably not been able to observe. When I began to work in psychoanalytic group therapy, I realized for the first time the resistance to listening to women who had had this type of very serious problem. For example, in a group in which there were men and women, men who had carried out all kinds of perversions,—even murder and all kinds of extreme violent acts—, could not listen to a woman who said she felt like she wanted to kill her child.

In 1981, it occurred to me to bring together a group with two types of patients, those who had committed acts of incest or sexual molestation and those who had been victims, without these cases being directly connected. The perpetrators, the abusers, had suffered some kind of abuse themselves, but when they arrive to be treated, no one has any kind of empathy for them, all the empathy and sympathy is directed towards the victims. At times this situation totally blinds us and prevents us from appreciating the need abusers have in their therapy to understand themselves. This can be seen a lot with patients who have terrorized their victims. I imagine that in Peru some of this has been done, right?

Yes, but not much.

I remember that when I was there, I supervised a colleague who had worked on this.

There is a center that is working with the victims, but I do know that in Rwanda this kind of thing has been done.

And in South Africa, in a center that is called Retribution. Of course, psychoanalytic group therapy is intense, it is quite difficult, and carried out with these patients is even more difficult. I think it requires a fairly sophisticated training to do it well, and in addition you have to have supervision or what I call "intervision" that is the supervision between colleagues with the same type of experience. The process begins with a phase of patient preparation that I describe in the book that I have just published, and it turns out that it is invaluable for those who have been in abusive relationships, as perpetrators or victims or as both.

If we have a group of victims solely, generally a situation of excessive sympathy and empathy arises, in which patients cannot freely express their feelings of revenge, anger, and hatred. On the other hand, in a mixed group of victims and perpetrators, the expression of these feelings is very easily reached. It is very important to be able to express feelings of revenge because it allows there to be a link, or a very particular bond with the victim of abuse, and when that person can experience rage it can be seen as a good thing. When they are still in the revenge phase, we know that there is a connection from which they have not been able to liberate themselves. The psychoanalytic group therapy also offers a unique opportunity to see the therapist facilitating independence, that can be achieved as a result of the group. There is no evidence of this in individual therapy. I think that group therapy is invaluable and reliable for patients with perversions and also in cases of sexual abuse.

It's like when it is said that only a thief can catch a thief. The therapist uses the understanding that the perverse has of others like him or her as a tool.

Exactly, you have said it so clearly that it requires no further explanation. For some time now, I have been working on a concept that I call "malignant bonding". This type of bond was seen in a very tragic and frightening manner in a case that occurred here a few years ago, the case of the West family. This family was made up of a married couple with children who lived in the north, in quite a populated area, but no one ever noticed when family members started to go missing, that there were things that were happening in the house next door. This was a couple who had children, male and female, and who dedicated themselves to doing all sorts of sadistic acts against them, especially against the daughters and even against the female friends of the daughters. They had devised a very sophisticated system for seduction and then torture and murder of the children, who they buried in their own house. It was a domestic family holocaust, that nobody noticed for years, until finally someone noticed that something was wrong and only then did the authorities intervene and discover that this family had done all kinds of appalling things and that in addition many of them had been planned by the woman. The existence of a malignant bonding between husband and wife was then acknowledged.

The recognition of this dreadful bond began years before with the case of the murderers of the Moors in the north of England, the case of Myra Hindley and her partner Ian Brady, in which the participation of the woman was evident. How could the active participation of the woman be proven?

Because the atrocities they perpetrated were recorded, the cries of the children who they tortured and then murdered. In court they listened to the children begging Myra, "Please, don't do this to me!" It was proven that the woman was not another of her partner's victims, in fact she had been the one who had designed the types of torture. They were both imprisoned. He committed suicide in prison a few weeks later, she is still alive.

Recently we have been able to observe the case of a couple of young people who were 19 or 20 years old who were in charge of baby-sitting a 3-month-old niece, on whom they carried out all kinds of sexual abuse. They were discovered because they were caught on film. This is because for this type of person it is not enough to carry out their atrocities but they also had to record them on video so they could be repeated. This was what struck me the most in the account by Norberto Marucco at the Congress of the International Psychoanalytical Association in Berlin, where his understanding of embryonic repetition was clear. He did not speak of cases of perversion, but it really caught my attention.

Of course, these are very, very extreme cases. However, I have seen very similar cases at the clinic. For example, I had a patient who was unable to accept that her husband was doing all kinds of terrible sexual things to girls in the horse-riding classes he gave. She felt she was not very appreciated sexually by her husband because he would tell her that he was going to take the little girls sexually and he was going to make a film. She felt like a kind of femme fatale and she cared very little that first the girls' breasts were touched and then the vagina. She began to experience sexual satisfaction, especially when she watched the films. It took her a while to realize that her husband was a pedophile and that the only way she could sexually satisfy him was to do these types of performances. At the same time, she became aware of her own sexual stimulation and her own perversion. This is why she came for a consultation and the case was discovered. A while afterwards I was asked to give my expert opinion in family court.

I am fully immersed in this topic of malignant bonding because I think it is very important to establish that it is about two people who have a kind of radar that attracts them to each other in a secret relationship that the two share and that entails having been sexually abused and has to do with being sexually stimulated. They are led unknowingly to these acts. Once they start talking, and an intimacy between them is established so that they discover each other's secrets, the taboo no longer exists. They then have to create another taboo situation, like experiencing a sexual relationship together, of the two of them torturing, terrorizing, and eventually sexually abusing children under their care. This then becomes the most incredible taboo and they have to record everything so they are able to repeat it compulsively.

Does recording it guarantee control?

It guarantees control when you see it or listen to it again. In that moment the sense of control is reinitiated, they put themselves again in the role of perpetrators.

Does this have something to do with the case of the Catholic institutions in Ireland, Belgium, or Germany, in which the priests who cared for the children abused them or is this another type of perversion?

It is a similar problem, but I don't think it has to do with them being Catholic or not, although Catholics are involved, and they have the trigger of celibacy. I've seen this a lot, and with great surprise in England, in centers dedicated to the care of children who have been abused in their home or who have been abandoned. As a society we have to accept our share of the responsibility. We all feel great indignation when we realize that the caregivers of these children abuse them sexually, but we are unaware that it is a very poorly paid type of job that has no type of training or supervision. This makes them magnetic foci for this type of person. That is to say, we not only put children in situations of risk but also the caregivers themselves. We should be much more careful and have greater social responsibility regarding this type of situation.

You're saying there's a social collusion.

That's right, a social collusion in which each time there is great wonder when a case comes to light.

There is a saying "Even the just may sin with an open chest of gold before them". We are putting vulnerable children in situations of risk because we place them in the care of people with no adequate training.

Exactly. At the moment, the abusers are the ones spoken about, and not the abused. Why are there children who are abused and others who are not abused? We never look closely at the profile of the abused child. In therapy groups I have seen that the abused girl or the abused boy feels a lot of shame, perhaps of themselves because they have felt a kind of sexual satisfaction. When they can face their family after being in therapy, one of their brothers or sisters invariably tells them that the father or mother had also approached them and that they had refused. Then the child who has been abused feels doubly betrayed because something has happened to them that has allowed them to collude with their abuser.

Why is there this difference? Because there are children who are more vulnerable because of what happened to them at birth, because of how they were received, all these very complex situations that are not that easy to delimit. For example, I think group therapy is essential for those who have been victims of incest. It is very important that this type of patient also works individually because if not, the situation of being provoked by the adult partner arises.

Have you managed to convey this and influence in some way how people think in our profession?

I think so. I have former students who are now colleagues who are developing and even deepening my work and who are writing many books. I feel very proud of them. One piece of perhaps more tangible proof is that the Tavistock and the Portman have dedicated one day in May 2008 to the celebration of the 20 years of the publication of my book *Mother, Madonna, Whore* with people who came from the United States, Israel, Germany, Belgium, etc. Besides, many of my ex-students presented their work, done my way but gone into more depth by them. Not only was it a day of great pride for me, but a volume of the *British Journal of Psychotherapy* from May 2009 was dedicated to my work, including my lectures and the lectures of other colleagues who were influenced by my work.

In addition, the International Association for Forensic Psychotherapy, of which I was founding member, then president, and now honorary president for life, is consolidating itself more and more. The importance of forensic psychotherapy is that it is not the function of a single professional but requires the participation of diverse professionals: people who do art therapy or music therapy, nurses, social workers, police, teachers... The teachers and police officers are perhaps the ones who have the first contact with situations of abuse or antisocial behaviors. They have to be fortified with emotional and intellectual tools to deal with them and be part of a professional network to warn about and prevent these cases. I believe that it is also very important to educate people and education can be done via newspapers, magazines, all kinds of media.

Do you have media activity?

Yes, this Sunday something has come out in one of the newspapers that is nationally circulated. Every year we also have a publication of everything that was done the previous year.

Your work is focused on clinical activity. I was wondering if you feel you can contribute, for example, to the understanding of political violence?

I think all the problems of violence are related. As you know, John Alderdice, who works in this field, attends our congresses. I instigated a meeting between him and James Gilligan, and they still see each other and work together. Everything that precedes violence is rooted in humiliation, a subjective humiliation. We can see it all the time in the conflict in Ireland or in the Israeli-Palestinian conflict and elsewhere. All of them have felt humiliated and the feeling of being mistreated, and they want to have vengeance. Everything is linked to social injustice. This can be seen in the domestic sphere, where women can feel very humiliated by the lack of emotional and intellectual support, making them feel very inferior to men, and when they are alone, they respond with a form of violence towards children. We also see it in political movements that they feel unfairly treated. We see it every day. In London, for example, despite it being a very cosmopolitan city, nationalist movements can be seen. The same in Italy, with its huge influx of African migration. Those who feel persecuted migrate to other places with the hope of it not being the same, though on occasion they move to places where they will be even more persecuted. We all have some responsibility for making some people feel very humiliated. Do you remember Britten's opera, *Billy Budd*? It clearly shows how humiliation towards a great boy who stuttered but showed no malice can lead him to murder someone.

I use these kinds of artistic examples a lot to help people to understand. For example, to deal with the subject of sadomasochism in a couple I refer to the movie *The Night Porter,* with Dirk Bogarde. This is a man who has been a member of the Gestapo, and of a Jewish girl in a concentration camp in which there have been two types of exchange. In one he is a key abuser and she subjects herself to acts of sexual abuse. At that moment it is seen as a survival strategy, but at the beginning of the film it can be seen that she and her husband, who is the director of the opera and who has received all kinds of praise and awards, arrive to a hotel where Dirk Bogarde works as a doorman. It can be seen from the beginning that when guests arrive they are very important, he has a kind of obsequiousness and that when he addresses others who are below him he shows great contempt and a kind of arrogance. When she arrives, it is clear that it would be very easy for her to humiliate him, but something unexpected happens. After seeing and recognizing each other, the situation leads to the repetition of what happened in the concentration camp. It all ends with their deaths as the only way to survive this horrible situation of sadomasochism.

Now, this would be, in some way, as if Nazism itself were a perversion transformed into a social structure, if I understood you.

Yes, exactly.

It is institutionalized perversion, transformed into a cultural apparatus.

You've made me remember that some years ago I wrote an article on this, "The institutionalization of perversion", in which I asked myself if the torturers were perverse. I remember having been in Peru and having had that conversation. The people talked about whether the torturers were perverse and in that moment, I thought that it was an insult to the perverse, because the torturers had not only been trained to do what they did, and they do not just eventually get a type of sexual satisfaction by doing so, it also has earned them the respect of other people and they did it like a job.

I understand that there can be a sexual pervert who is honest and never accept being a torturer.

Look, I remember a patient of mine who was a policeman and an exhibitionist. As a police officer he would go to the parks to punish and humiliate other exhibitionists, he used perversion to make money. But look at how guilt works. This patient was discovered exposing himself two days before completing 25 years of working as a policeman, which left him automatically without any type of retirement. That is, he punished himself in a totally decisive way. If they had discovered it three days later nothing would have happened to him because he would have already had the money for his retirement.

I also had as a patient a nun who had done everything to be discovered, but she was seen as such an innocent person, so pure, that even when she worked in the church she stole a lot of money that was meant for alms, she was never discovered. She had to go to the police and confess what she had done, because if not no-one would have discovered what she did, which is how she ended up as a patient. That is, sometimes there are situations that can facilitate the perversion of a person, but the feeling of guilt will be such that they will expose themselves.

And our profession? It could be very attractive to the perverse...

Of course, that is why it is mandatory for us to undergo a psychoanalysis for so many years. Our curiosity, our desire to know more about the psyche, can also lead to some type of abuse without realizing it.

On one occasion I was with a patient who told me that he needed to be humiliated, to be thoroughly punished with all kinds of instruments of torture, so he could obtain sexual satisfaction. But he also told me that he could not listen, that he could not hear very well, that he was a little deaf. I suddenly realized that I was yelling at him loudly. I realized that if I was loud enough so he could hear me a colleague outside was going to say I was punishing him with my tone of voice and from then on, I had to change everything. I realized that I had become a kind of partner of his perversion, since he had also told me that he was interested in a nurse and I realized that I was collaborating with his perversion. Even though I had a lot of experience, I had been taken in by the situation.

This is why I think it's very important to always have supervision and a space to be able to talk about all kinds of issues that we may feel. We know that there are many colleagues who have found themselves in very shameful situations, like sleeping with their patients. We have found ourselves in totally ignoble situations and so repeating the traumatic situations where the problems originated.

I will change the subject completely to touch on a more personal aspect. How have you found the experience of having a granddaughter and how do you relate to her?

I think becoming a grandparent, a grandmother, is a very pleasant experience, but I think it is a field that should be explored much more than it has been, it has not been researched very much at all. I also believe it is a different experience depending on your social status or on the country you are in, or even if you're grandfather to your son's son or if you are a grandmother to your daughter's daughter. There is also a big difference between being a grandfather or a grandmother, they are very different cases, completely different. I have written a paper on it.

Now I think there is a change, I see it mainly in Western countries. I do not know to what extent it happens in other places, but there is a change that is taking place and it is a welcome one, there is a different role now than what it used to mean to be a grandmother. Before, when a grandchild was born, the role of the grandmother was to be with the daughter all the time and take care of everything. Then would come the father, a bit like a visitor, but the boy or girl would be more accustomed to being with the mother and the grandmother. Now, we as parents, I refer to our generation, I think we've done our job well. We had to teach our sons to take care of more 'feminine things', to understand femininity and motherhood more, and to take on a more active fatherhood. The role that the mother-in-law or the grandmother had, the father now has. Now he is present from birth, which means that the child has the deep relationship with the mother, so much so that at first, he or she sees the mother or her breasts as part of themselves, and the child also has a bond with the father. The father now changes diapers and does many of the things that our fathers and our husbands did not do. Now chores are shared with the mother, and the grandmother is a little more left out.

Some American sociologists call this "halo parenting", that is, an extended family that is not only the nuclear family but that includes the grandparents. The grandfather almost always has less emotional investment than the grandmother. He is always a little more withdrawn, more of an observer. I think however that the most important role of the grandmother begins when the child's socialization starts, around 7, 8 or 9 months old. Before this, the child gets on very well with the mother and sees the father as the third part in a benign triangulation. Later on, another person becomes visible in the family circle, a grandmother, for example, and the child sometimes resents this other figure that appears and disrupts the relationship with his mother and then with his father. After 9 months, when everything begins to be much more recognizable, the action of the grandparent or grandmother, who can provide help without the child's rejection is more important. At this point the grandmother should be prepared for it. I think there should be groups of grandmothers and grandfathers, I think that there is material on this to write a book. It is a much-needed topic, and a few colleagues and I have been thinking about it. When the role of the grandmother is held by the mother-in-law, she always plays the role of the witch, whereas the grandmother is the good one.

But the mother-in-law is also the grandmother.

Exactly, do you realize what I'm saying? The mother-in-law is the one who becomes a type of monster because she is interfering with the couple, the grandmother does not, because she is a person who comes to help. It is the same person, but the issue of motherhood separates them. The grandfathers and the grandmothers must be more prepared to endure a lot of frustration. I do not believe that everything is great joy and shared satisfaction, sometimes, they don't want to share either.

And your experience with your own granddaughter?

My experience with my granddaughter has taught me that I have to be a little on the outside, but I also have to provide everything. I have a room in my house decorated for her, so she knows when she wants she can come over. I go to wait for her one day a week after school and take her to music class, then to dinner. I also have her at home on some weekends and I take her to the theater or to the opera. She is 6 years old, but I've been doing this for some time. This way though, like every grandmother, one has to put up with not being the 'first' person, the first person is the mother. Sometimes I think that in this generation parents need their children more than children need their parents, and I think that the fun of being a grandparent is that you can get up to mischief with the child and sometimes I even put myself on par with my granddaughter's age. Her parents sometimes get upset and challenge me for not being a person who educates her, but I am the person that gets into mischief.

It's as if the parents would like the grandmother to be part of the control, of the education, and what the grandmother does is to become an accomplice.

Accomplice of the girl and accomplice in mischief. For example, these days nobody gives sweets to children and it is the grandmother who gives them chocolate. Of course, the parents are very much against this.

I was wondering if there is not some kind of revenge of the grandmother against her daughter.

But they say that one of the functions of the grandparent is to spoil the grandchildren.

You feel like an accomplice of your granddaughter.

Yes. For example, one day she started crying a little hysterically and I told her. "No, with me no hysteria, delinquency yes, but no hysteria."

I read that the English are now giving rights to the grandparents, something that does not exist anywhere else in the world. In primitive cultures the grandparents had the role of guardians.

And in Eastern cultures too.

But only in England do they have legal rights. Do you know how this came about?

No, I think it's because of the conflict that existed between parents who were getting a divorce. At that point the grandparents expected to play the role of substitute parents, but I'm not sure if that's why.

Because I think it's an interesting idea.

But, for example, it's also fun if you say the opposite. There is a place and a space to listen for everything. In the program I told you about on Radio 4, "Woman's Hour", I heard some grandmothers who said some really unexpected things: "I already had enough with my own children, I don't want to have any more problems with my grandchildren, I have no interest in caring for grandchildren, I want to be free, to dedicate myself to my profession". I find it very interesting that women can talk openly about not wanting to have anything to do with their grandchildren.

Of course, it's freedom, professional development, whatever.

Exactly. Why should they not be able to speak that way without being judged.

What projects do you have for the future?

Well, I'm doing many things right now. I'm working in different countries, giving lectures. For example, I discovered that there is a very good book called *La Mamá Mala*, written by some Italians many years ago, but that has never been translated. It gives me so much satisfaction to know that there are attempts to try to understand these women more, because they suffer a lot. It has made me think that in fact my last book is very academic, so I have a project to make a popular version without so many bibliographical references, without quotations from authors, so that it can reach all kinds of people.

Great, anything else you'd like to add?

Well there are many clinical things that I would like to talk about. My work is full of clinical things. By the way, a new edition of my book *Mother, Madonna, Whore* has just been published in Argentina by Editorial Planeta. It is a much better translation than the previous one and it has three new chapters and a very interesting prologue by Horacio Etchegoyen, to whom I owe most of the things that I have done professionally.

Estela Welldon with her son and her father

Konstantin Nemirovsky, ex-student of Estela Welldon's first forensic psychotherapy course class on a visit to London with his wife, their daughter, & Estela herself. Konstantin Nemirovsky created a similar course in Moscow.

Estela Welldon with Horacio Etchegoyen

Estela Welldon with Arlene Kramer Richards

Estela Welldon with Arnold D. Richards

Estella Welldon in her Office

Estela Welldon with Otto Kernberg on the occasion of her Honorary Fellowship to the American Psychoanalytic Association, awarded on January 2014

Estela Welldon's Afterword

My first choice of a professional career was my yearning to become a teacher. I clearly remember as an 8-year-old child "teaching" reading and writing to my younger friends with the help of a blackboard and chalk. But it is not just coincidence that my eventual vocation, becoming a doctor, was connected to my brother's sudden death at age 13, when I was 11. He died, because of his doctor's misdiagnosis. By that age I was already passionate about social injustice, so my professional choice then became deeply imbued with my wanting to become a psychiatrist – a medical specialty that is, at heart, a form of teaching.

As a doctor, I have spent my professional life studying and applying, the science of medicine. As a psychiatrist, I have spent my time contemplating the depths of the human psyche – sometimes in despair but usually in wonderment. As a psychotherapist, I have continually been drawn to 'the beauty hidden within the ugly'.

Was I lucky or perhaps extremely strong headed?

Perhaps in trying to understand social injustice, intimate injustice, domestic violence, and violence of all sorts, we may be able to achieve an understanding which could lead us to heightened creativity and fewer acts of violence.

Let me be clear, the effects of abuse are terrible and can be long lasting, but condemnation and abhorrence will not change behavior or provide the help those victims need.

Our therapeutic work is hard, but it is the only solution.

I have always felt very honoured to have been able to help people in distress and I have learnt over the years that the only way to help these people is to understand their suffering.

I learned of this extreme predicament through my own personal pain and emotional distress. You see, we almost always automatically identify with the victim--and almost never with the aggressor-perpetrator.

It is obvious that a lack of understanding of a crime leads us to punish it. D.W. Winnicott taught us that the antisocial tendency is linked inherently with deprivation and that criminal actions and offences always imply a sense of hope. In some sense, we might add, that criminal actions and offenses are the product of creative as well as violent states of mind. Winnicott was able to understand that so many acts of violence are committed by those who feel ignored, and forgotten, and that recognizing this might help us understand the full force of the trauma not just the loss but a complete absence and denial of any recognition as a human being.

I have often observed rescue fantasies and wishes for reparation in people who embark on this sort of work. It is then that I ask myself, "Have they all experienced some kind of emotional trauma which consciously or unconsciously they feel the need to metabolize?" How many of those of us who feel driven into these professions have experienced not only severe traumatic losses, but also a great sense of helplessness and impotence in dealing with family disturbances, which have created a desire for reparation? I mean by this a need to achieve an internal sense of justice for whatever was felt as an inflicted pain, from the inside or outside, over which we had no control.

In this particular field, where awareness of unconscious processes is crucial, we must be humble enough to acknowledge the importance of external factors and not just internal ones. At times we felt, just as our patients do almost all the time, too wounded to adjust to a "normative" development or too angry to compromise and to settle down into what would have been considered a safer or more amenable profession. I have also wondered whether these "safer" professions would have left us frustrated and irritated; we might have found them "futile" and "trivial". It may be our need to feel on the edge that makes it possible for us to believe that our lives are worthwhile.

My book *Mother, Madonna, Whore: The Idealization and Denigration of Motherhood*, first published in 1988, described for the first time an awareness of the problems that women experience throughout motherhood, including pregnancy, childbirth, and in the process of looking after their babies at all stages of their development. The book had an enormous impact and 20 years after its publication the Tavistock and Portman Clinics dedicated a day to celebrate its publication and to recognise the contribution it had made to transforming the clinical care offered by services working with mothers and their babies.

But perhaps the most insightful acknowledgement at the time of its publication was what Professor Paul Verhaegen wrote:

"Putting forward the combination between motherhood and perversion made Estela famous - to my knowledge, she is the first clinician who has demonstrated time and again that perversion can only be understood if we look at the mother, meaning that we have to reconsider female perversion as well. The importance of this clinical insight cannot be overrated, and it testifies to three things. First of all, to her intellectual courage. Secondly, to her sense of humanity. And last but not least, to her clinical finesse.

To publish a book about motherhood as the seat of perversion in a feminist time and place is just another way of trying to commit suicide by proxy. With hindsight, it is almost a miracle that the book was actually published and read. It goes against two visceral certainties: that mothers are always saints and that women are never perverse. Estela confronts us with another reality, not caring about being politically correct, as long as it is clinically correct. And correct she was and is - beyond the romantic mainly boyish ideals of a saint motherhood and the feverish phallic masculine ideals of a sexy femininity, there are real women with real problems that are totally different from both the romantic and the erotic universe of the male, but it takes courage to put that forward against both traditional patriarchal and then contemporary feminist views."

Paul Verhaeghe, 2008

Mother, Madonna, Whore has never been out of print and has since been translated into many different languages, including Italian, German and Spanish. The increasing awareness of this important work prompted people from many different countries to invite me to give lectures, teach, and attend a wide variety of international meetings.

In 1990 I created the course in Forensic Psychotherapy at the Portman Clinic, and through this I was able to realize my childhood dream of teaching. Many well-known and influential clinicians and academics graduated from this course. I am proud to say that the alumni include many illustrious and influential clinicians and academics.

In 1991, with the aim of changing perceptions and creating an understanding, I founded the International Association for Forensic Psychotherapy, which built a platform and a forum for professionals working around the world in this field to gather once a year to discuss in a frank and honest environment our own difficulties encountered in our daily work dealing with abuse and abusers. I am honored to have been given the role of Honorary President for Life.

In 1997 together with my friend and colleague Dr. Cleo van Velsen we published *Forensic Psychotherapy: The Practical Approach*. We observed with curiosity that most professionals working with offender patients were women, so much so that we made a decision that all chapters would be written by women. This produced an uproar amongst our male colleagues who were already indignant that we had established a "forensic women's dinner club" to which men were not invited, which involved a periodic visit to the Groucho Club (of which I am a founding member) for social meetings followed by dinner.

This outcry was especially voluble as in the UK such clubs had typically been founded by men and tended to not to allow women membership.

I have been told that one of my greatest contributions has been on the social level, in creating communities of colleagues and keeping them together over decades and decades.

Since then I have published a number of other books including *Sadomasochism* (2002), *Playing with Dynamite: A Personal Approach to the Understanding of Perversions, Violence and Criminality* (2011) translated into 3 languages, *Sex Now, Talk Later* published by Karnac (2016) and *Sadomasochism in Arts and Politics* (2016).

In this way forensic psychotherapy began to develop, extend and to grow strongly in many different countries, some of which have developed their own associations, as in Italy, Austria, and Russia. I am very grateful to Konstantin Nemirovsky, who started in Moscow, the Russian course for Forensic Psychotherapy of which I am the director. In the Summer of 2020, a new initiative by Nemirovsky created the Summer School of Forensic Psychotherapy with Russian students attending the course. It has grown beyond my wildest dreams and in July the Russian summer school program will take take place in London.

It has been extremely gratifying to see how this new discipline has grown especially in countries in which an understanding of anti-social criminal action is much needed.

I have been awarded a number of honours in my lifetime, including in 1997 a D.Sc. Honorary Doctorate of Science by Oxford Brookes University, in 2014, being made an Honorary member of the American Psychoanalytic Association for my work in helping to understand women who harm children, and then in June 2018 being made a visiting International Professor at Universidad Católica Lima Peru.

At the end of 2018, I was taken by surprise and delighted to discover that many of those clinicians who as youngsters had completed the course in Forensic Psychotherapy had together, led by Professor Brett Kahr, written and collated a set of essays about the ways in which they had taken ideas, concepts and formulations that I had developed through my own clinical work with offending patients, and extended them in their own work. The fact that I had not suspected such a book in the least made me feel that perhaps I'm not such a good forensic psychiatrist after all, but also attests to their skilful insights into the perfect deceit! Even my own son, whose photography adorns the cover of these collected articles, hadn't revealed the ruse. I was so enthralled by the book that I went home and immediately read throughout the night until the sunrise reminded me of my fatigue. I was especially moved by those beautiful chapters written by colleagues Gill McGauley and Alan Corbett, who are no longer with us, whom I, and I know others, miss with deep affection. The book was and still is a great revelation and a wonderful journey down memory lane, abundant with our dialogues and conversations. It made me feel extremely proud and I felt it as a monument to our collaborative efforts to push forward the horizons of forensic psychotherapy.

In 2019, the first edition of the *The International Journal of Forensic Psychotherapy*, a marvellous collaboration between the International Association for Forensic Psychotherapy and Phoenix Publishing House emerged. I regard its birth as the culmination of my most ambitious, lifetime project – the creation of a new profession of forensic psychotherapy that provides a fantastic opportunity to share our knowledge and expertise worldwide to improve the treatment of the most antisocial, delinquent criminals in the most effective and humane ways possible.

In late 2019, I was again surprised and hugely honoured to be awarded a PPNow (Psychoanalytic Psychotherapy Now) Lifetime Achievement award by the British Psychoanalytic Council.

All of my work has been in the service of improving the lives of those who have entered the criminal justice system and to enable us to better help them regain their lives and prevent further criminal actions.

It saddens me that throughout much of my professional life, the emphasis has always been placed on the offence rather than on the offender, and, moreover, that attention has been devoted to punishment rather than to treatment. Indeed, any attempts at a psychodynamic understanding of offenders and their delinquent actions have been marginalized or ignored completely.

When, as members of the public, we become confronted by acts of violence, through the clever wording of newspapers and other forms of media, we become bombarded by seemingly odd and bizarre acts of cruelty. Our automatic response tends to be one of shock, disbelief and, most worryingly, condemnation. Hearing about, or reading about, acts of criminality often result in a loss of our usual intellectual capacities. We become a bit stupid, ignorant, judgemental, and devoid of any sense of discernment. Rather than attempting to understand the origins of forensic pathology, we make fun of offenders as "weird" or "disgusting" and we condemn them and think no more about what they have done or *why*.

I believe it is vital that we look at ourselves and at our own reactions so that we can begin to understand the true nature of antisocial acts, particularly when they include a sexual component, which many find difficult to comprehend. We certainly do need to understand the unconscious "reasons" for a person's activities; also, we must better comprehend the origin of condemnation by society at large. By endeavouring to appreciate the causes of forensic activities, and, also, by studying the reactions of ordinary citizens, we have an opportunity to provide greater insight and more compassionate care. Only through such understanding will we be able to *rehumanize* the already *dehumanized*.

Forensic psychotherapy is a relatively new discipline. Our aims include not only the re-humanization of the perpetrator but, also, the complete psychodynamic understanding of such individuals. By bringing together the fields of forensic psychiatry, forensic psychology, and psychoanalytical psychotherapy, we have an opportunity to combine the best of all of these disciplines, regardless of the seriousness of the offence, in order to comprehend the conscious and unconscious motivations of the criminal mind. In doing so, we seek neither to condone nor to condemn. On the contrary, the aim of forensic psychotherapy is to help the offender to acknowledge his or her responsibility for such acts and thereby help to save the offender and society at large from the further perpetration of crimes.

The more we come to understand about the offender, the greater will be the opportunities for positive preventative action. This, in turn, can lead to better management and to the implementation of more cost-effective treatments for our patients.

Forensic psychotherapy requires its practitioners to become sensitive to the needs of the patient, the needs of society at large, and our own needs as practitioners, in terms of supervision, self-care, and further training and support. Such treatment of the forensic patient should be carried out, ideally, within the National Health Service and not within the private sector. And we must recognise that while we work with the criminal justice system, we do not always have the same goals; we prioritise treatment and rehabilitation.

It is crucial to remember that, while championing treatment alongside containment of violent offenders, we cannot work in isolation. The forensic psychotherapist must work as part of a team. We cannot undertake this work in a heroic solo fashion. Healing begins with referral agencies, which include the courts of justice. Thus, inevitably, our work involves a large number of people. The forensic psychotherapist must feel safely and securely contained in caring and unobtrusive surroundings. Institutions should provide such structures in order to protect the therapists from the inherent anxiety produced by such work.